St. Louis Cardinals 2019

A Baseball Companion

Edited by Patrick Dubuque, Aaron Gleeman and Bret Sayre

Baseball Prospectus

Craig Brown and Dave Pease, Consultant Editors
Rob McQuown and Harry Pavlidis, Statistics Editors

Copyright © 2019 by DIY Baseball, LLC.
All rights reserved

This book or any part thereof may not be reproduced or transmitted in any form or by any means, electronic or mechanical, including photocopying, recording, or by any information storage and retrieval system, without permission in writing from the publisher.

Limit of Liability/Disclaimer of Warranty: While the publisher and the author have used their best efforts in preparing this book, they make no representations or warranties with respect to the accuracy or completeness of the contents of this book and specifically disclaim any implied warranties of merchantability or fitness for a particular purpose. No warranty may be created or extended by sales representatives or written sales materials. The advice and strategies contained herein may not be suitable for your situation. You should consult with a professional where appropriate. Neither the publisher nor the author shall be liable for any loss of profit or any other commercial damages, including but not limited to special, incidental, consequential, or other damages.

Library of Congress Cataloging-in-Publication Data:
paperback
ISBN-13: 978-1-949332-56-8

Project Credits
Cover Design: Kathleen Dyson
Interior Design and Production: Jeff Pease, Dave Pease
Layout: Jeff Pease, Dave Pease

Baseball icon courtesy of Uberux, from https://www.shareicon.net/author/uberux

Ballpark diagram courtesy of Lou Spirito/THIRTY81 Project, https://thirty81project.com/

Manufactured in the United States of America
10 9 8 7 6 5 4 3 2 1

Table of Contents

Foreword v
    Rob Mains

Statistical Introduction vii

Part 1: Team Analysis

Table for Two: Previewing the 2019 St. Louis Cardinals 3
    Bill Thompson and Matthew Trueblood

Performance Graphs 7

2018 Team Performance 8

2019 Team Projections 9

Team Personnel 10

Busch Stadium Stats 11

Cardinals Team Analysis 13

Part 2: Player Analysis

Cardinals Player Analysis 20

Cardinals Prospects 97

Part 3: Featured Articles

The Hole in The Shift is Fixing Itself 111
    Russell Carleton

The State of the Quality Start 115
    Rob Mains

Heads-Up Hacking—The First Pitch 121
    Matthew Trueblood

A Hymn for the Index Stat 127
    Patrick Dubuque

Index of Names 131

Foreword

Rob Mains

Welcome to this companion of the 2019 St. Louis Cardinals. We at Baseball Prospectus are excited to provide this analysis of the Cardinals.

Our website, Baseball Prospectus, is a leader in delivering high-quality commentary and data to baseball fans everywhere. To some, those words—commentary and data—appear mutually exclusive. There are people out there who believe that traditional analysis and advanced analytics must run on different paths. But the simplistic narrative of stats vs. traditionalists just isn't true. Every team's analytics department interacts with scouting, development, and major league operations with a common goal: Delivering a championship. New technologies, like radar tracking of pitch speeds and movement, enable talent evaluators to focus on qualitative aspects of pitching like mechanics and pitch sequencing. In-game strategies like infield shifts, based on batters' hit tendencies, help turn balls in play into outs. Hitters use information to adjust their swings to maximize run production.

All these numbers can seem, at best, intimidating, and at worst, counterproductive to the casual fan. Even as technology and analysis have embedded themselves deeply into the way teams run, it can often feel like statistics create a displacement between the viewer and the sport, breaking them out of the action. And yet every fan incorporates the numbers to some degree; stats like batting average and earned run average, so fundamental to how we talk about performance, are actually complicated formulas. They don't bother people because those formulas have become second nature, as easy to translate as the action on the field.

Along the way, new statistics have entered baseball's lexicon. You'll see some of them, like on-base percentage (which measures a batter's ability to get on base via walk, hit batter, or hit), OPS (on-base plus slugging), and average exit velocity (the speed of balls off a hitter's bat) on broadcasts. Others, like DRC+, might well be new to you. Some of them have been well-defined to the public, others haven't. That lack of context has created ambiguity. Fans know that a ball hit 100 mph is scorched, but does that mean extra bases? (Not if it's hit on the ground or high in the air it doesn't.)

St. Louis Cardinals 2019

For those who are amenable to them, the new statistics can increase the enjoyment and understanding of the game. They can help fans identify when a pitcher is tiring, when a stolen base or a bunt attempt makes sense (and, more often, when it doesn't), or how a team's lineup might be constructed. Websites like Baseball Prospectus add to that understanding by weaving metrics into the narrative of the game. That's the goal of this publication: to take some of the newer, more complicated statistics and make them as intuitive as the ones on the back of old baseball cards.

But you don't need to love analytics to love baseball. The fans at BP who worked together to write this guide are captivated first and foremost by the game itself. We're drawn to Aaron Judge's power, Francisco Lindor's glove, Billy Hamilton's speed and Patrick Corbin's slider and don't need numbers to tell us why they're so mesmerizing. The underlying statistics provide depth to the game that we all love.

We hope you'll find that this guide helps you better understand the Cardinals. Our analysts have studied the team's major league personnel and its minor league affiliates to identify their strengths and weaknesses, both the obvious ones and those that only a careful dissection of players' performances—yes, including the data—can reveal. You don't need us to tell you who was good and who wasn't in 2018, but our models and writers can help you project how each player is going to perform this year and beyond, and appreciate the greatness of each new game as it unfolds. As in the sport itself, the human and analytic components combine to generate a deeper overall understanding.

Think back to the first time you saw a baseball game on a high-definition TV. You'd grown familiar with how the game looked and felt on a picture tube. But new TV allowed you to see details that you'd never seen before. That's how advanced statistics work. The game itself is why you're here and why you're buying this. (And, for that matter, why we wrote it.) The statistical measures provide the sharper focus, the detail, the depth of knowledge that you didn't have before, generating an overall superior picture. Enjoy the view.

—Rob Mains is an author of Baseball Prospectus.

Statistical Introduction

Sports are, fundamentally, a blend of athletic endeavor and storytelling. Baseball, like any other sport, tells its stories in so many ways: in the arc of a game from the stands or a season from the box scores, in photos, or even in numbers. At Baseball Prospectus, we understand that statistics don't replace observation or any of baseball's stories, but complement everything else that makes the game so much fun.

What stats help us with is with patterns and precision, variance and value. This book can help you learn things you may not see from watching a game or hundred, whether it's the path of a career over time or the breadth of the entire MLB. We'd also never ask you to choose between our numbers and the experience of viewing a game from the cheap seats or the comfort of your home; our publication combines running the numbers with observations and wisdom from some of the brightest minds we can find. But if you *do* want to learn more about the numbers beyond what's on the backs of player jerseys, let us help explain.

Offense

At the end of this past year, we've revised our methodology for determining batting value. Long-time readers of Baseball Prospectus will notice that we've retired True Average in favor of a new metric: Deserved Runs Created Plus (DRC+). Developed by Jonathan Judge and our stats team, this statistic measures everything a player does at the plate–reaching base, hitting for power, making outs, and moving runners over–and puts it on a scale where 100 equals league-average performance. A DRC+ of 150 is terrific, a DRC+ of 100 is average, and a DRC+ of 75 means you better be an excellent defender.

DRC+ also does a better job than any of our previous metrics in taking contextual factors into account. The model adjusts for how the park affects performance, but also for things like the talent of the opposing pitcher, value of different types of batted-ball events, league, temperature, and other factors. It's able to describe a player's expected offensive contribution than any other statistic we've found over the years, and also does a better job of predicting future performance as well.

The other aspect of run-scoring is baserunning, which we quantify using Baserunning Runs. BRR not only records the value of stolen bases (or getting caught in the act), but also accounts for a runner's ability to go first to third on a single or advance on a fly ball.

Defense

Where offensive value is *relatively* easy to identify and understand, defensive value is ... not. Over the past dozen years, the sabermetric community has focused mostly on stats based on zone data: a real-live human person records the type of batted ball and estimated landing location, and models are created that give expected outs. From there, you can compare fielders' actual outs to those expected ones. Simple, right?

Unfortunately, zone data has two major issues. First, zone data is recorded by commercial data providers who keep the raw data private unless you pay for it. (All the statistics we build in this book and on our website use public data as inputs.) That hurts our ability to test assumptions or duplicate results. Second, over the years it has become apparent that there's quite a bit of "noise" in zone-based fielding analysis. Sometimes the conclusions drawn from zone data don't hold up to scrutiny, and sometimes the different data provided by different providers don't look anything alike, giving wildly different results. Sometimes the hard-working professional stringers or scorers might unknowingly inflict unconscious bias into the mix: for example good fielders will often be credited with more expected outs despite the data, and ballparks with high press boxes tend to score more line drives than ones with a lower press box.

Enter our Fielding Runs Above Average (FRAA). For most positions, FRAA is built from play-by-play data, which allows us to avoid the subjectivity found in many other fielding metrics. The idea is this: count how many fielding plays are made by a given player and compare that to expected plays for an average fielder at their position (based on pitcher ground-ball tendencies and batter handedness). Then we adjust for park and base-out situations.

When it comes to catchers, our methodology is a little different thanks to the laundry list of responsibilities they're tasked with beyond just, well, catching and throwing the ball. By now you've probably heard about "framing" or the art of making umpires more likely to call balls outside the strike zone for strikes. To put this into one tidy number, we incorporate pitch tracking data (for the years it exists) and adjust for important factors like pitcher, umpire, batter, and home-field advantage using a mixed-model approach. This grants us a number for how many strikes the catcher is personally adding to (or subtracting from) his pitchers' performance ... which we then convert to runs added or lost using linear weights.

Framing is one of the biggest parts of determining catcher value, but we also take into account blocking balls from going past, whether a scorer deems it a passed ball or a wild pitch. We use a similar approach–one that really benefits from the pitch tracking data that tells us what ends up in the dirt and what doesn't. We also include a catcher's ability to prevent stolen bases and how well they field balls in play, and *finally* we come up with our FRAA for catchers.

Pitching

Both pitching and fielding make up the half of baseball that isn't run scoring: run prevention. Separating pitching from fielding is a tough task, and most recent pitching analysis has branched off from Voros McCracken's famous (and controversial) statement, "There is little if any difference among major-league pitchers in their ability to prevent hits on balls hit in the field of play." The research of the analytic community has validated this to some extent, and there are a host of "defense-independent" pitching measures that have been developed to try and extricate the effect of the defense behind a hurler from the pitcher's work.

Our solution to this quandary is Deserved Run Average (DRA), our core pitching metric. DRA looks like earned run average (ERA), the tried-and-true pitching stat you've seen on every baseball broadcast or box score from the past century, but it's very different. To start, DRA takes an event-by-event look at what the pitchers does, and adjusts the value of that event based on different environmental factors like park, batter, catcher, umpire, base-out situation, run differential, inning, defense, home field advantage, pitcher role, and temperature. That mixed model gives us a pitcher's expected contribution, similar to what we do for our DRC+ model for hitters and FRAA model for catchers. (Oh, and we also consider the pitcher's effect on basestealing and on balls getting past the catcher.)

It's important to note that DRA is set to the scale of runs allowed per nine innings (RA9) instead of ERA, which makes DRA's scale slightly higher than ERA's. The reason for this is because ERA tends to overrate three types of pitchers:

1. Pitchers who play in parks where scorers hand out more errors. Official scorers differ significantly in the frequency at which they assign errors to fielders.
2. Ground-ball pitchers, because a substantial proportion of errors occur on grounders.
3. Pitchers who aren't very good. Better pitchers often allow fewer unearned runs than bad pitchers, because good pitchers tend to find ways to get out of jams.

Since the last time you picked up an edition of this book, we've also made a few minor changes to DRA to make it better. Recent research into "tunneling"–the act of throwing consecutive pitches that appear similar from a batter's point of view until after the swing decision point–data has given us a new contextual factor to account for in DRA: plate distance. This refers to the distance between successive pitches as they approach the plate, and while it has a smaller effect than factors like velocity or whiff rate, it still can help explain pitcher strikeout rate in our model.

New Pitching Metrics for 2019

We're including a few "new" pitching metrics for 2019's suite of Baseball Prospectus publications, but you may be familiar with them if you've spent time scouring the internet for stats.

Fastball Percentage

Our fastball percentage (FB%) statistic measures how frequently a pitcher throws a pitch classified as a "fastball," measured as a percentage of overall pitches thrown. We qualify three types of fastballs:

1. The traditional four-seam fastball;
2. The two-seam fastball or sinker;
3. "Hard cutters," which are pitches that have the movement profile of a cut fastball and are used as the pitcher's primary offering or in place of a more traditional fastball.

For example, a pitcher with a FB% of 67 throws any combination of these three pitches about two-thirds of the time.

Whiff Rate

Everybody loves a swing and a miss, and whiff rate (WHF) measures how frequently pitchers induce a swinging strike. To calculate WHF, we add up all the pitches thrown that ended with a swinging strike, then divide that number by a pitcher's total pitches thrown. Most often, high whiff rates correlate with high strikeout rates (and overall effective pitcher performance).

Called Strike Probability

Called Strike Probability (CSP) is a number that represents the likelihood that all of a pitcher's pitches will be called a strike while controlling for location, pitcher and batter handedness, umpire and count. Here's how it works: on each pitch, our model determines how many times (out of 100) that a similar pitch was called for a strike given those factors mentioned above, and when normalized for each batter's strike zone. Then we average the CSP for all pitches thrown by a pitcher in a season, and that gives us the yearly CSP percentage you see in the stats boxes.

As you might imagine, pitchers with a higher CSP are more likely to work in the zone, where pitchers with a lower CSP are likely locating their pitches outside the normal strike zone, for better or for worse.

Projections

Many of you aren't turning to this book just for a look at what a player has done, but for a look at what a player is going to do: the PECOTA projections. PECOTA, initially developed by Nate Silver (who has moved on to greater fame as a political analyst), consists of three parts:

1. Major-league equivalencies, which use minor-league statistics to project how a player will perform in the major leagues;
2. Baseline forecasts, which use weighted averages and regression to the mean to estimate a player's current true talent level; and
3. Aging curves, which uses the career paths of comparable players to estimate how a player's statistics are likely to change over time.

With all those important things covered, let's take a look at what's in the book this year.

Team Prospectus

You bought this book to learn more about your favorite (or maybe least-favorite, who are we to judge?) team, so let's talk about them. After a thoughtful preview of the 2019 season, you'll be presented with our Team Prospectus. This outlines many of the key statistics for each team's 2018 season, as well as a very inviting stadium diagram.

First you'll find the Performance Graphs page. The first is the 2018 Hit List Ranking. This shows our Hit List Rank for the team on each day of the 2018 season and is intended to give you a picture of the ups and downs of the team's season, including their highest and lowest ranks of the year. Hit List Rank measures overall team performance and drives the Hit List Power Rankings at the baseballprospectus.com website.

The second graph is Committed Payroll and helps you see how the team's payroll has compared to the MLB and divisional average payrolls over time. Payroll figures are currents as of January 1, 2019; with so many free agents still unsigned as of this writing, the final 2018 figure will likely be significantly different for many teams. (In the meantime, you can always find the most current data at Baseball Prospectus' Cot's Baseball Contracts page.)

St. Louis Cardinals 2019

The third graph is Farm System Ranking and displays how the Baseball Prospectus prospect team has ranked the organization's farm system since 2007. It also indicates the highest and lowest ranks that the farm system achieved over that time.

We start the Team Performance page with the squad's unadjusted and third-order 2018 win-loss records, presented in divisional context. We then list the three highest performing hitters and pitchers by WARP for 2018. Beneath that are a host of other team statistics. **Pythag** presents an adjusted 2018 winning percentage, calculated by taking runs scored per game (**RS/G**) and runs allowed per game (**RA/G**) for the team, and running them through a version of Bill James' Pythagorean formula that was refined and improved by David Smyth and Brandon Heipp. (The formula is called "Pythagenpat," which is equally fun to type and to say.)

Next up is **DRC+**, described earlier, to indicate the overall hitting ability of the team either above or below league-average. Run prevention on the pitching side is covered by **DRA** (also mentioned earlier) and another metric: Fielding Independent Pitching (**FIP**), which calculates another ERA-like statistic based on strikeouts, walks, and home runs recorded. Defensive Efficiency Rating (**DER**) tells us the percentage of balls in play turned into outs for the team, and is a quick fielding shorthand that rounds out run prevention.

After that, we have several measures related to roster composition, as opposed to on-field performance. **B-Age** and **P-Age** tell us the average age of a team's batters and pitchers, respectively. **Salary** is the combined team payroll for all on-field players, and Doug Pappas' Marginal Dollars per Marginal Win (**M$/MW**) tells us how much money a team spent to earn production above replacement level.

Ending this batch of statistics is the number of disabled list days a team had over the season (**DL Days**) and the amount of salary paid to players on the disabled list (**$ on DL**); this final number is expressed as a percentage of total payroll.

Next to each of these stats, we've listed each team's MLB rank in that category from 1st to 30th. In this, 1st always indicates a positive outcome and 30th a negative outcome, except in the case of salary–1st is highest.

The Team Projections page is intended to convey the team's operational capacity entering the 2019 season. We start with the team's PECOTA projected record for 2019, again in divisional context. The **+/-** column indicates how many more or less wins the team is projected to get than they got in 2018. We then list the three highest projected hitters and pitchers by WARP for 2018. A brief farm system summary follows, with the team's top prospect and number of BP Top 101 Prospects. Finally, we list the key new players and departed players, along with their 2019 projected WARP.

Alex Bregman 3B

Born: 03/30/94 Age: 25 Bats: R Throws: R
Height: 6'0" Weight: 180 Origin: Round 1, 2015 Draft (#2 overall)

YEAR	TEAM	LVL	AGE	PA	R	2B	3B	HR	RBI	BB	K	SB	CS	AVG/OBP/SLG
2016	CCH	AA	22	285	54	16	2	14	46	42	26	5	3	.297/.415/.559
2016	FRE	AAA	22	83	17	6	0	6	15	5	12	2	1	.333/.373/.641
2016	HOU	MLB	22	217	31	13	3	8	34	15	52	2	0	.264/.313/.478
2017	HOU	MLB	23	626	88	39	5	19	71	55	97	17	5	.284/.352/.475
2018	HOU	MLB	24	705	105	51	1	31	103	96	85	10	4	.286/.394/.532
2019	HOU	MLB	25	675	96	38	3	23	78	73	107	12	4	.272/.359/.463

Breakout: 6% Improve: 52% Collapse: 5% Attrition: 2% MLB: 100%
Comparables: Anthony Rendon, David Wright, Pablo Sandoval

YEAR	TEAM	LVL	AGE	PA	DRC+	VORP	BABIP	BRR	FRAA	WARP
2016	CCH	AA	22	285	172	38.9	.286	1.6	SS(51): -3.4, 3B(11): 1.4	2.7
2016	FRE	AAA	22	83	161	10.0	.333	-1.2	SS(14): 2.1, LF(3): -0.1	0.8
2016	HOU	MLB	22	217	107	9.6	.317	0.5	3B(40): 0.9, SS(6): -0.1	1.1
2017	HOU	MLB	23	626	114	34.7	.311	-1.5	3B(132): 8.7, SS(30): -2.9	3.9
2018	HOU	MLB	24	705	150	72.6	.289	-1.6	3B(136): 5.4, SS(28): -0.4	7.4
2019	HOU	MLB	25	675	125	37.3	.295	0.0	3B 7, SS 0	4.6

After the projections page, we share a few items about the team's home ballpark. There's the aforementioned diagram of the park's dimensions (including distances to the outfield wall), a few important biographical facts about the stadium, a graphic showing the height of the wall from the left-field pole to the right-field pole, and a table showing three-year park factors for the stadium. The park factors are displayed as indexes where 100 is average, 110 means that the park inflates the statistic in question by 10 percent, and 90 means that the park deflates the statistic in question by 10 percent.

Following the ballpark page, we have a **Personnel** section that lists many of the important decision-makers and upper-level field and operations staff members for the franchise, as well as any former Baseball Prospectus staff members who are currently part of the organization.

Position Players

After all that information and a thoughtful bylined essay covering each team, we present our player comments. Each player is listed with the major-league team who employed him as of early January 2019. If a player changed teams after that point via free agency, trade, or any other method, you'll be able to find them in the book for their previous squad.

First, we cover biographical information (age is as of June 30, 2019) before moving onto the stats themselves. Our statistic columns include standard identifying information like **YEAR**, **TEAM**, **LVL** (level of affiliated play) and **AGE** before getting into the numbers. Next, we provide raw, unstranslated numbers like you might find on the back of your dad's baseball cards: **PA** (plate appearances), **R** (runs), **2B** (doubles), **3B** (triples), **HR** (home runs), **RBI** (runs batted in), **BB** (walks), **K** (strikeouts), **SB** (stolen bases) and **CS** (caught stealing). Then we have unadjusted "slash" statistics: **AVG** (batting average), **OBP** (on-base percentage) and **SLG** (slugging percentage).

Just below the stats box is **PECOTA** data, which is discussed further in a following section. After that, it's on to a pithy and always-informative comment written by a member of the Baseball Prospectus staff, before we cover more stats.

The second text box repeats YEAR, TEAM, LVL, AGE, and PA, then moves on to **DRC+** (Deserved Runs Created Plus), which we described earlier as total offensive expected contribution compared to the league average. Next, one of our oldest active metrics, **VORP** (Value Over Replacement Player), considers offensive production, position and plate appearances. In essence, it is the number of runs contributed beyond what a replacement-level player at the same position would contribute if given the same percentage of team plate appearances. VORP does not consider the quality of a player's defense.

BABIP (batting average on balls in play) tells us how often a ball in play fell for a hit, and can help us identify whether a batter may have been lucky or not … but note that high BABIPs also tend to follow the great hitters of our time, as well as speedy singles hitters who put the ball on the ground.

The next item is **BRR** (Baserunning Runs), which covers all of a player's baserunning accomplishments which includes (but isn't limited to) swiped bags and failed attempts. Next is **FRAA** (Fielding Runs Above Average), which also includes the number of games previously played at each position noted in parentheses. Multi-position players have only their two most frequent positions listed here, but their total FRAA number reflects all positions played.

Our last column here is **WARP** (Wins Above Replacement Player). WARP estimates the total value of a player, which means for hitters it takes into account hitting runs above average (calculated using the DRC+ model), BRR and FRAA. Then, it makes an adjustment for positions played and gives the player a credit for plate appearances based upon the difference between "replacement level"¬–which is derived from the quality of players added to a team's roster after the start of the season¬–and the league average.

Catchers

Catchers are a special breed, and thus they have earned their own separate box which displays some of the defensive metrics that we've built just for them. As an example, let's check out J.T. Realmuto.

YEAR	TEAM	P. COUNT	FRM RUNS	BLK RUNS	THRW RUNS	TOT RUNS
2016	MIA	18935	-8.5	1.8	2.1	-5.6
2017	MIA	18959	5.3	1.7	1.0	9.1
2018	MIA	16399	-0.4	0.9	0.1	0.4
2019	PHI	18448	-1.4	1.5	0.7	0.8

The **YEAR** and **TEAM** columns match what you'd find in the other stat box. **P. COUNT** indicates the number of pitches thrown while the catcher was behind the plate, including swinging strikes, fouls, and balls in play. **FRM RUNS** is the total run value the catcher provided (or cost) his team by influencing the umpire to call strikes where other catchers did not. **BLK RUNS** expresses the total run value above or below average for the catcher's ability to prevent wild pitches and passed balls. **THRW RUNS** is calculated using a similar model as the previous two statistics, and it measures a catcher's ability to throw out basestealers but also to dissuade them from testing his arm in the first place. It takes into account factors like the pitcher (including his delivery and pickoff move) and baserunner (who could be as fast as Billy Hamilton or as slow as Yonder Alonso). **TOT RUNS** is the sum of all of the previous three statistics.

Pitchers

Let's give our pitchers a turn, using 2018 NL Cy Young winner Jacob deGrom as our example. Take a look at his first stat block: the first line and the **YEAR**, **TEAM**, **LVL** and **AGE** columns are the same as in the position player example earlier.

Here too, we have a series of columns that display raw, unadjusted statistics compiled by the pitcher over the course of a season: **W** (wins), **L** (losses), **SV** (saves), **G** (games pitched), **GS** (games started), **IP** (innings pitched), **H** (hits allowed) and **HR** (home runs allowed). Next we have two statistics that are rates: **BB/9** (walks per nine innings) and **K/9** (strikeouts per nine innings), before returning to the unadjusted **K** (strikeouts).

Next up is **GB%** (ground ball percentage), which is the percentage of all batted balls that were hit in the ground, including both outs and hits. Remember, this is based on observational data and subject to human error, so please approach this with a healthy dose of skepticism.

BABIP (batting average on balls in play) is calculated using the same methodology as it is for position players, but it often tells us more about a pitcher than it does a hitter. With pitchers, a high BABIP is often due to poor defense or bad luck, and can often be an indicator of potential rebound, and a low BABIP may be cause to expect performance regression. (A typical league-average BABIP is close to .290-.300.)

After a witty 150ish words on the player like only Baseball Prospectus's staff can provide, it's on to that second stat block, which repeats the YEAR, TEAM, LVL, and AGE columns. The metrics **WHIP** (walks plus hits per inning pitched) and **ERA**

St. Louis Cardinals 2019

(earned run average) are old standbys: WHIP measures walks and hits allowed on a per-inning basis, while ERA measures earned runs on a nine-inning basis. Neither of these stats are translated or adjusted.

DRA (Deserved Run Average) was described at length earlier, and measures how many runs the pitcher "deserved" to allow per nine innings. Please note that since we lack all the data points that would make for a "real" DRA for minor-league events, the DRA displayed for minor league partial-seasons is based off of different data. (That data is a modified version of our cFIP metric, which you can find more information about on our website.)

Jacob deGrom   RHP
Born: 06/19/88   Age: 31   Bats: L   Throws: R
Height: 6'4"   Weight: 180   Origin: Round 9, 2010 Draft (#272 overall)

YEAR	TEAM	LVL	AGE	W	L	SV	G	GS	IP	H	HR	BB/9	K/9	K	GB%	BABIP
2016	NYN	MLB	28	7	8	0	24	24	148	142	15	2.2	8.7	143	47%	.312
2017	NYN	MLB	29	15	10	0	31	31	201[1]	180	28	2.6	10.7	239	48%	.305
2018	NYN	MLB	30	10	9	0	32	32	217	152	10	1.9	11.2	269	48%	.281
2019	NYN	MLB	31	13	9	0	31	31	186	145	18	2.3	10.7	221	46%	.286

Breakout: 8%   Improve: 29%   Collapse: 28%   Attrition: 6%   MLB: 85%
Comparables: Erik Bedard, A.J. Burnett, CC Sabathia

YEAR	TEAM	LVL	AGE	WHIP	ERA	DRA	WARP	MPH	FB%	WHF	CSP
2016	NYN	MLB	28	1.20	3.04	3.30	3.5	96.3	59.6	12.1	47.2
2017	NYN	MLB	29	1.19	3.53	3.02	5.7	97.2	55.5	14.5	49.5
2018	NYN	MLB	30	0.91	1.70	2.09	8.0	98.2	52.1	16.3	48.4
2019	NYN	MLB	31	1.02	2.91	3.23	3.9	96.6	54.5	14.8	48.2

Just like with hitters, **WARP** (Wins Above Replacement Player) is a total value metric that puts pitchers of all stripes on the same scale as position players. We use DRA as the primary input for our calculation of WARP. You might notice that relief pitchers (due to their limited innings) may have a lower WARP than you were expecting or than you might see in other WARP-like metrics. WARP does not take leverage into account, just the actions a pitcher performs and the expected value of those actions … which ends up judging high-leverage relief pitchers differently than you might imagine given their prestige and market value.

MPH gives you the pitcher's 95th percentile velocity for the noted season, in order to give you an idea of what the *peak* fastball velocity a pitcher possesses. Since this comes from our pitch tracking data, it is not publicly available for minor-league pitchers.

Finally, we display the three new pitching metrics we described earlier. **FB%** (fastball percentage) gives you the percentage of fastballs thrown out of all pitches. **WhiffRt** (whiff rate) tells you the percentage of swinging strikes induced out of all pitches. **CS Prob** (called strike probability) expresses the likelihood of all pitches thrown to result in a called strike, after controlling for factors like handedness, umpire, pitch type, count, and location.

PECOTA

All players have PECOTA projections for 2019, as well as a set of other numbers that describe the performance of comparable players according to PECOTA. All projections for 2019 are for the player at the date we went to press in early January and are projected into the league and park context as indicated by the team abbreviation. All PECOTA projected statistics represent a player's projected major-league performance.

The numbers beneath the player's stats–Breakout, Improve, Collapse, Attrition–are part and parcel of the PECOTA projections. They estimate the likelihood of changes in performance relative to the player's previously-established level of production, based on the performance of comparable players:

Breakout Rate is the percent change that a player's production will improve by at least 20 percent relative to the weighted average of his performance over his most recent seasons.

Improve Rate is the percent chance that a player's production will improve at all relative to his baseline performance. A player who is expected to perform just the same as he has in the recent past will have an Improve Rate of 50 percent.

Collapse Rate is the percent chance that a position player's production will decline by at least 25 percent relative to his baseline performance.

Attrition Rate operates on playing time rather than performance. Specifically, it measures the likelihood that a player's playing time will decrease by at least 50 percent relative to his established level.

Breakout Rate and Collapse Rate can sometimes be counterintuitive for players who have already experienced a radical change in performance level. It's also worth noting that the projected decline in a player's rate performances might not be indicative of an expected decline in underlying ability or skill, but could just be an anticipated correction following a breakout season.

MLB% is the percentage of similar players who played in the major leagues in their relevant season.

The final pieces of information are the player's three highest-scoring comparable players as determined by PECOTA. All comparables represent a snapshot of how the listed player was performing at the same age as the current player, so if a 23-year-old pitcher is compared to Bartolo Colon, he's actually being compared to a 23-year-old Colon, not the version that pitched for the Rangers in 2018, nor to Colon's career as a whole.

St. Louis Cardinals 2019

A few points about pitcher projections. First, we aren't yet projecting peak velocity, so that column will be blank in the PECOTA lines. Second, projecting DRA is trickier than evaluating past performance, because it is unclear how deserving each pitcher will be of his anticipated outcomes. However, we know that another DRA-related statistic–contextual FIP or cFIP–estimates future run scoring very well. So for PECOTA, the projected DRA figures you see are based on the past cFIPs generated by the pitcher and comparable players over time, along with the other factors described above.

Lineouts

In each chapter's Lineouts section, you'll find abbreviated text comments, as well as most of same information you'd find in our full player comments. We limit the stats boxes in this section to only including the 2018 information for each player.

Exclusive Player Visualizations

In our constant battle to provide you with new and interesting baseball content you can't find anywhere else, we've added a trio of data visualizations to each hitter's entry in these books and a pair of visualizations for each pitcher.

For hitters, you'll find three new infographics. The first is each player's **Batted Ball Distribution**, which displays the five major sections of the field: LF (left), LCF (left center), CF (center), RCF (right center), and RF (right). The percentage indicated tells us what percentage of batted balls from that hitter fell within that part of the field during the 2018 season. We've also included the hitter's slugging percentage on balls in play (also called **SLGCON**) for that part of the field.

You'll also see two heatmaps: **Strike Zone vs LHP** and **Strike Zone vs RHP**. These heat maps represent a view of the strike zone from behind the catcher. Areas where there is a darker coloration represent the places where a higher percentage of pitches resulted in hits. In other words, the heatmap represents a hitter's "sweet spots" for getting hits against either left-handed or right-handed pitchers, depending on the image.

Pitchers get two images that help explain what their pitches look like from a hitter's perspective: **Pitch Shape vs LHH** and **Pitch Shape vs RHH**. These images show you the shape and the "tunneling" effect of each pitcher's offerings from the batter's perspective. For each type of pitch that a pitcher throws (represented by an indicator shape), there's a set of dots indicating the flight path, where each dot represents a 0.01-second interval. This maps the average trajectory and speed of an offering, ending where the ball crosses the plate. The solid black box represents the regular strike zone, while the gray contour lines indicate the range of locations that a pitcher typically works in.

Below the image, we provide a bit more detailed information about each pitcher's average offering in the **Pitch Types** box. Here, we also list each of the pitcher's major offerings under the **Type** column.

- **Fastballs** (which usually refers to the four-seam variation)
- **Sinkers** and/or two-seam fastballs
- **Cutters** (which could include "hard" cutters like cut fastballs and "soft" cutters that resemble hard sliders)
- **Changeups** (not including most splitters)
- **Splitters** (split-fingered pitches, forkballs, and some split-changes)
- **Sliders** and/or slurves
- **Curveballs** (including spike-curveballs and knuckle-curveballs, as well as some slurvy curves)
- **Slow curveballs** and/or eephus pitches
- **Knuckleballs**
- **Screwballs**

The **Freq** column indicates the percentage of overall pitches that fall into each of those type categories; if a pitcher has a 16.55% score for changeups, then that's the percent of all pitches that he throws as changeups. **Velo** is exactly what you think it is: the average miles per hour for each pitch type. **H Mov** is the number of inches of horizontal movement on the average pitch of that type, while **V Mov** is the number of inches of vertical movement on the average pitch of that type. (At Baseball Prospectus, we measure this over the long flight of the ball and include gravity into the V Mov number in order to give you the most realistic representation of what the pitch *actually* does.)

If you're wondering about the second number in brackets, that's the index for that velocity or movement compared to the league average. Like DRC+, a score of 100 means that the speed or movement is about the same as league average, while a higher score means that there's higher velocity or movement than the league average. Numbers below 100 indicate less velocity or movement than the league average.

Part 1: Team Analysis

Table for Two: Previewing the 2019 St. Louis Cardinals

Bill Thompson and Matthew Trueblood

MATT TRUEBLOOD: Three Octobers without bunting being hung at Busch Stadium seems to have stirred the Cardinals to action a bit. It's pretty easy to love the Paul Goldschmidt and Andrew Miller additions, but I'm left to wonder: was it enough? Should they have pushed harder for Harper, or was that fit a poor one? Do you have any nits to pick with either of the big acquisitions?

BILL THOMPSON: It's hard to think of Bryce Harper being a poor fit, especially when he'd be sliding into Dexter Fowler's right field spot. It seems like the Cards are banking on Yairo Muñoz to be their main defensively-oriented backup outfielder. That is, well, kind of scary when his 2018 adventures in the outfield produced an FRAA of -7.5. Harper would have been another big acquisition that would have helped them in a division that appears to be headed towards an outright dog fight. Perhaps, though, we should be asking about what the Cards didn't do to help support their actual big acquisitions?

MATT: Yeah, it's interesting: I think the organization feels like Goldschmidt and Miller are capstones for a roster that can win as otherwise constructed. It certainly seems like they want to keep Tyler O'Neill's path to playing time relatively free, although as you note, Fowler complicates even that. I think O'Neill is a good enough athlete to handle center when needed and an above-average defender in the corners. PECOTA adores his power profile, and pegs him for a .231 ISO that would match its projection for his batting average. The problem is, dude made contact on 53.9 percent of his swings last year; no other player has made contact less than 56 percent of the time in a season. They actively chose to replace Randal Grichuk with O'Neill, and now it looks like O'Neill is roughly a poor man's Grichuk.

That's emblematic of their approach to the winter on the pitching side, too. They elected not to go get a starter, and there are a bunch of good options there, but I sense they're higher on some of these hurlers than I would be. How do you view the rotation?

BILL: I'm big on their rotation; I think it gets slept on far too much. Wainwright and Wacha are good as end-of-the-line guys, and honestly, that's all they'll ever need from them. A main three of Martínez, Mikolas, and Flaherty is dangerous.

St. Louis Cardinals 2019

68.5 is the DRA- for Flaherty in 2018, and it seems like most people have forgotten just how good he was for the team last year. Obviously, they need Martínez to bounce back to his pre-2018 form, and that's certainly possible. Between injuries and clubhouse stuff last year, he was never able to get it going. Now that he's not the ace, Martínez is someone I think will be able to get back to what made him capable of three straight years of a DRA- below 77. That's without even mentioning Alex Reyes, who if he can show he is ready to handle any sort of workload, could push Wainwright out of the rotation.

Their rotation will be a strength, but even with the addition of Miller I have questions about their bullpen. Who do you see being able to step up in that pen?

MATT: I'll name two guys: Jordan Hicks, and Dakota Hudson. Those aren't exactly big secrets, but they're the keys to St. Louis's season, I think. Hicks is famous for throwing hard, but the truth of the matter is that he doesn't miss nearly enough bats with that heat to warrant the hype. What he needs to do is throw his slider (which *does* miss bats; opponents whiffed on 52.3 percent of swings against it last year!) about twice as often as he currently does.

Hudson might only need to adjust to the role of relief pitcher and start thinking dominant thoughts. There's a reason he's been named Pitcher of the Year in his leagues at the two highest levels of the minors over the last two seasons.

Let me turn the focus back to the position players. Who's your guy? Who breaks out and changes the game for them this season?

BILL: They traded for him for a reason: It has to be Goldschmidt. He's an elite defender, decent on the basepaths for a first baseman, and his hit tool remains among the best in the league. Together with Rizzo, Votto, and Aguilar the NL Central is truly a murderer's row of first basemen. It's been a long time since St. Louis had a player at Goldschmidt's level. He's the given though, it's others who will have to step up to help him and Carpenter power the offense.

He wasn't acquired in a trade this year, but Marcell Ozuna was their biggest acquisition last year and is still sneaky good. PECOTA projects him for a DRC+ of 118, and if he can just manage to be a little better in the field and make better decisions on the basepaths he can be worth more than his projected 2.7 WARP. Ozuna can step up: He is that type of talent, and this is the year I think he takes that final step towards being more than just potential.

On the other side of the spectrum, is there anyone among the position players who you feel is due for significant regression? If so, do you see anyone in the Cards system that is ready to replace him?

MATT: Harrison Bader, Harrison Bader, Harrison Bader. It's remarkable that, basically after matriculating to the majors, he realized he can play the game faster than he ever played it in the minors. His utterly unrestrained style is so much fun. That said, he swings pretty freely, that swing is pretty grooved (so he can't reliably spoil pitches on which he's fooled), and he still struggles to identify spin. There are plenty of guys who could take over for him if he goes backward—Jose Adolis Garcia, Randy Arozarena, the aforementioned O'Neill—but his defense is irreplaceable, and he's the guy they're betting on.

Yadier Molina will never fade, though. As long as he's the nerve center of this team, they'll still win occasional games through sheer force of will, high baseball IQ, and infuriatingly consistent clutch hitting. [Sets up card table, sits down in folding chair] Change my mind.

BILL: I learned my lesson quite a while ago when it comes to the current President of the Hall of Very Good. It doesn't matter that he's too old, too slow, or that he's been around too long. He's still a very good player who manages to get key hits or throw out runners at the most inopportune time possible for the other team. Old Yadi is a walking billboard for the righteousness of Cardinals Devil Magic.

It always astounds me that the Cardinals manage to find actual devil magic players every year. Yadi is, of course, actually a very good player who should be irreplaceable. But, were he to get injured you just know that this team would find some guy in low A named James McNotacatcher who would go on to lead the league in batting average with the bases loaded and throwing runners out from his knees with his eyes closed. It is utterly insane to me how the Cardinals defy all logic and scouting every year by bringing up dudes who should not be able to contribute, but end up being game changers for the team.

Although, maybe this year will be different now that the managerial genius that is Mike Matheny is completely out of the picture and the Redbirds are now under Mike Shildt's guidance for a whole season. Does he have some devil magic in him, or is he going to be a little too in over his head in a tight NL Central race?

MATT: That's the right question, if not (perhaps) how I'd have phrased it. It gets to the identity of this team—their exceptional record of player development and internal scouting. They win by always edging above their median projections, at individual and team levels, and by always being a bit deeper and better than people believed them to be.

Shildt's impact on that process, it seems to me, will only be positive. He handles a bullpen pretty well. He's an experienced manager (unlike, for instance, his predecessor). He seems to relate to his environment, including the players, coaches, and media members who occupy it, in a much healthier way. This organization has not done what it's done over the last 20 years by accident; they're genuinely brilliant. They'll continue to get the most out of guys like DeJong, Hicks, and Jack Flaherty. They're going to get more from Lane Thomas and Genesis Cabrera than you think they should. Ultimately, I think they'll take a small step forward, because they have a person helming the ship now who understands where it's going and how it's supposed to get there.

So you're ok with Molina. Is there anyone you're less confident in? Anyone poised to take the kind of step backward this roster can't afford?

St. Louis Cardinals 2019

BILL: Framing it as taking a step back is kind of a misnomer, it's more the guys who are going to continue to slowly regress. Fowler, Wong, Gyorko, Wainwright, Cecil, etc. The Cards have some quality first-line players, but it's when you scroll further down the pecking order that it's easy to see this team missing the playoffs. All of the guys I mentioned have either been on a steady decline, or have held true to below average forms the past few years. That's putting a lot of pressure on Molina, Goldschmidt, Mikolas, Miller, etc. And, even then, Miller is a question mark because of injuries. I'm not convinced he's done, but I can't really argue against his track record of injuries the past few years continuing to hamper his performance come 2019. That's a real possibility, just like it's a real possibility that your top 6 or so guys perform up to expectations, but the next tier doesn't and the Cards fall just short of the playoffs as a result.

I think a more important question for the Cardinals is if any of the second tier players don't step up, is their upper core enough to get them to the playoffs in a division that seems intent on devouring itself? I say no, but I'm all ears as to how the Cardinals could end up making the playoffs with just the same guys being the go-to guys again this year.

MATT: Are the go-to guys really the same? Goldschmidt adds a ton of stability to the top of the lineup, projecting for a higher DRC+ (141) and a better WARP (5.4) than any Cardinal put up last season. Jack Flaherty only made 28 starts in the majors, and in 10 of those, he threw fewer than 90 pitches. The Cardinals went 11-17 in those games, but I think they'll win more of his starts than they lose in 2019. Whatever you think of Miller (and PECOTA still believes in him, projecting 0.8 WARP in just 56 innings), he's a more reliable backend option than Greg Holland was. The bullpen is, in general, more stable.

Look, there's a lot of downside risk here. You have to wonder about the mental and physical spaces Ozuna and Carlos Martinez are in. Michael Wacha's a year from free agency and coming off another injury-truncated season. Carpenter, Fowler, Molina, Goldschmidt, Wainwright, Miller, they could all go over the edge of an aging cliff.

I think they'll stay on the tightrope. I'm gonna predict 89 wins and a long (by St. Louis standards) awaited playoff berth. What's your call?

BILL: I'm far more sold on the Cards in 2019 than I have been since the 2015 season. I do like the additions, and I like the roster depth they have. I may have questions about all of it coming together, but that's true for all teams. In the end, I think more than enough comes together and they ride their rotation and the Goldschmidt-Carpenter duo to 91 wins and an NL Central crown. They'll get some more of that bunting, and if that rotation is the force I think it can be, maybe even an extra banner or two.

Performance Graphs

2018 Hit List Ranking

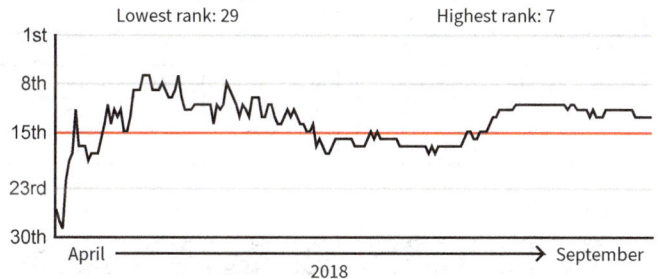

Committed Payroll (in millions)

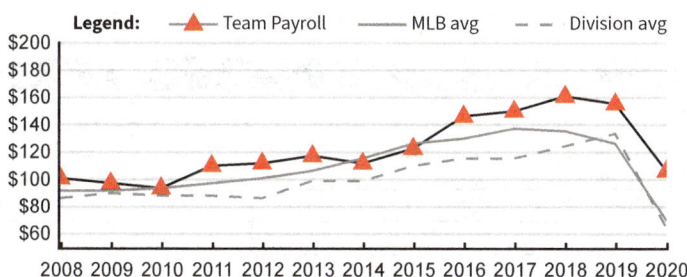

Farm System Ranking

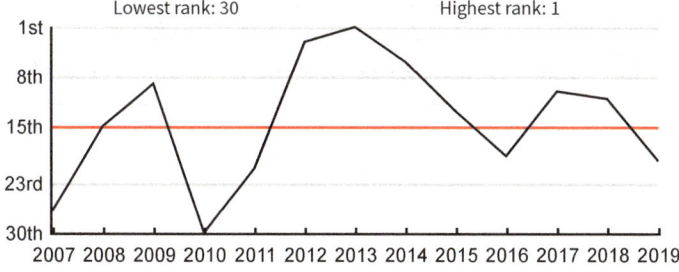

2018 Team Performance

ACTUAL STANDINGS

Team	W	L	Pct
MIL	96	67	.588
CHN	95	68	.582
SLN	**88**	**74**	**.543**
PIT	82	79	.509
CIN	67	95	.413

THIRD-ORDER STANDINGS

Team	W	L	Pct
MIL	93	70	.570
CHN	92	71	.564
SLN	**83**	**79**	**.512**
PIT	78	83	.484
CIN	71	91	.438

TOP HITTERS

Player	WARP
Matt Carpenter	4.6
Yadier Molina	3.1
Paul DeJong	2.7

TOP PITCHERS

Player	WARP
Miles Mikolas	4.5
Jack Flaherty	3.9
John Gant	1.6

VITAL STATISTICS

Statistic Name	Value	Rank
Pythagenpat	.544	12th
Runs Scored per Game	4.69	9th
Runs Allowed per Game	4.27	13th
Deserved Runs Created Plus	98	12th
Deserved Run Average	4.38	17th
Fielding Independent Pitching	3.93	9th
Defensive Efficiency Rating	.707	13th
Batter Age	28.2	18th
Pitcher Age	26.4	1st
Salary	$159.7M	10th
Marginal $ per Marginal Win	$3.7M	16th
Disabled List Days	$1,251.0M	17th
$ on DL	27%	27th

2019 Team Projections

PROJECTED STANDINGS

Team	W	L	Pct	+/-
MIL	88	74	.543	-8
SLN	**85**	**77**	**.524**	**-3**
CIN	81	81	.500	+14
PIT	80	82	.493	-2
CHN	79	83	.487	-16

TOP PROJECTED HITTERS

Player	WARP
Paul Goldschmidt	5.4
Matt Carpenter	4.0
Yadier Molina	2.6

TOP PROJECTED PITCHERS

Player	WARP
Jack Flaherty	2.8
Alex Reyes	2.0
Miles Mikolas	1.8

FARM SYSTEM REPORT

Top Prospect	Number of Top 101 Prospects
Alex Reyes, #21	2

KEY DEDUCTIONS

Player	WARP
Carson Kelly	1.5
Luke Weaver	1.3
Tyson Ross	0.3
Bud Norris	0.3

KEY ADDITIONS

Player	WARP
Paul Goldschmidt	5.4
Andrew Miller	0.9
Drew Robinson	0.4

Team Personnel

President, Baseball Operations
John Mozeliak

General Manager
Mike Girsch

Assistant General Manager
Moises Rodriguez

Manager
Mike Shildt

BP Alumni
Zach Mortimer
Christopher Rodriguez
Mauricio Rubio

Busch Stadium Stats

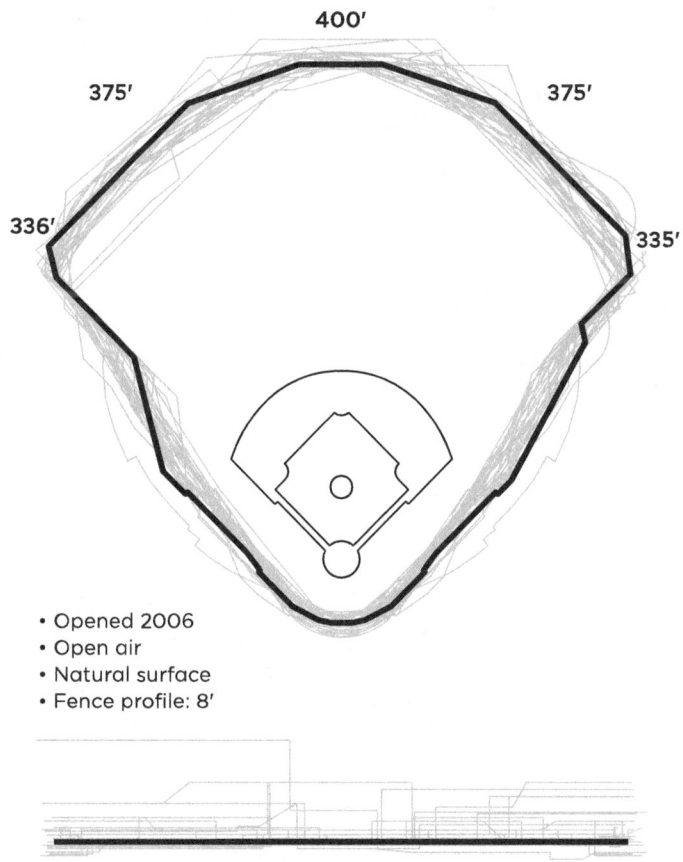

- Opened 2006
- Open air
- Natural surface
- Fence profile: 8'

Three-Year Park Factors

Runs	Runs/RH	Runs/LH	HR/RH	HR/LH
96	95	100	91	101

Cardinals Team Analysis

Flash back to the warm glow of 2011. The Cardinals had just won the World Series, surely not suspecting that it would be the last time that they did so for a while. Cardinals fans know what happened next. Albert Pujols, a man who had spent most of the previous decade winning MVPs, terrorizing opposing pitchers, and authoring a career already worthy of the Hall of Fame, was a free agent. At the time, he was about to enter his age-32 season, but was coming off a season in which he had produced 6.3 WARP.

What if the Cardinals had signed just signed Albert Pujols? The conventional wisdom is that the Cardinals dodged a bullet when they let Pujols decamp for the West Coast, and that Pujols's contract is now one of the most un-tradeable assets in baseball. There had even been talk that the Angels would release him before his contract expired. He still has 20 HR power, but with a sub-.300 OBP and limited defensive and baserunning value, he's starting to look like the kind of guy who would be replaced quickly if he were making $500,000.

Here's Pujols's contract that he actually signed with the Los Angeles, California Angels of Anaheim, California, and the WARP that he's produced since then.

Year	Salary	WARP
2012	$12,000,000	4.0
2013	$16,000,000	2.1
2014	$23,000,000	2.8
2015	$24,000,000	2.6
2016	$25,000,000	1.1
2017	$26,000,000	-1.8
2018	$27,000,000	0.5
2019	$28,000,000	?
2020	$29,000,000	?
2021	$30,000,000	?
2022-2031	$10,000,000 (personal services contract)	--

Let's go back in time and erase the word "Angels" on that contract and replace it with "Cardinals." How might recent Cardinal history have been different? It's a question that gets harder to answer the further that we get from 2012, when Pujols's contract with the Angels started. After all, a baseball team is an array of moving parts, and when you change one piece, the effects ripple through the system. It is fortunate for us that the Cardinals began their post-Pujols era by doing something which was obviously meant as a 1-to-1 compensatory move.

2012

On December 23rd, 2011, the Cardinals signed Carlos Beltrán to a 2-year contract and slid him into right field. Fortunately for this exercise, his salaries in 2012 and 2013 ($13 million in both years) are pretty close to what Pujols got from the Angels. In the meantime, regular Cardinals 2011 right fielder Lance Berkman grabbed a first baseman's glove from Pujols's vacated locker returning to a spot that had been his primary hangout since 2005. At least that was the plan. Berkman eventually hurt his knee in 2012 and only appeared in 32 games for the Cardinals. It's impossible to know whether Berkman would have been injured if he had been patrolling right field while Pujols had been stretching for infield throws at first. We know from Berkman's 2011 performance that he probably would have been a below average right fielder, but his performance at first base in what parts of 2012 (and eventually, 2013 and 2014) he did play shows that his defense at first wasn't much better.

Berkman's injury did reveal Allen Craig to the world—this was back when Allen Craig actually got MVP votes—and had Pujols been on the roster, Craig would have likely played in a corner outfield position. Advanced defensive metrics rated Craig as a somewhat below average first baseman in 2012 (and 2013), but slightly worse still in the outfield. The Cardinals probably would have lost some value there.

Verdict: In 2012, had the Cardinals signed Albert Pujols, they likely wouldn't have signed Carlos Beltrán (2.8 WARP for the year), and would have lost some of Allen Craig's defensive value. Compared to Pujols's 4.0 WARP, the Cardinals came out losers by something like 1.5 to 2 wins. Giving those two wins back to the 88-74 Cardinals wouldn't have made much difference in the standings. They still would have visited Atlanta for the Wild Card game (which they won), and the Nationals in the NLDS (which they won). Could Pujols, rather than Beltrán, have won them the extra game against the Giants in the NLCS that they would have needed to make the World Series? It's at least plausible that the answer is "yes."

2013

In 2013, for the second straight year, Carlos Beltrán made $13,000,000 and provided 2.8 WARP for the Cardinals. This time, under-earning Pujols by $3 million and out-performing him by 0.7 WARP. The biggest "moves" that the Cardinals made in the 2012-13 offseason involved signing lefty reliever Randy Choate (0.2 WARP) and utility guy Ty Wigginton (-0.6 WARP in 63 PA!) to contracts which paid them a combined $4 million in 2013. There's your cost-savings from not signing Pujols.

In the "signed Pujols" world, again, Beltrán, Choate, and Wigginton would have been elsewhere, with Allen Craig likely in a corner outfield spot for most of the season. But the biggest casualty of the counterfactual would have been Matt Adams, who emerged as the Cardinals' first baseman of choice (and actually did push Craig to the corners) while providing 1.1 WARP in value. Had Pujols been on the cold corner, the Cardinals would have likely been forced to use either Craig or Adams strictly in a pinch hitting role. It's reasonable to say that the Cardinals ended up a win or so better off for the fact that Albert Pujols wasn't there.

Verdict: The Cardinals had the best record in the National League in 2013 and made the World Series. Removing a win of value from that team by re-inserting Albert Pujols probably doesn't derail that train, but it wouldn't have helped. In the same wishy-washy way that Pujols might have helped the Cardinals a bit in 2012, he probably would have hurt the Cardinals a bit in 2013.

2014 and 2015

Now, we begin the post-Beltrán era of Cardinals history and the era where Fat Albert started to have a particularly fat contract ($23 million in 2014; $24 million in 2015). We also begin the part of the exercise where it's harder to nail down what moves the Cardinals made because they weren't committed to paying Albert Pujols that money. Other players (and their salaries) had since come off the books and some of the surrounding cast had changed. The closest thing to a replacement for Beltrán that the Cardinals committed to on the free agent market was Jhonny Peralta who checked in at a tidy $15 million salary in 2014 and 2015. Peralta responded by putting up 4.4 and 4.1 WARP in those seasons, respectively, besting Pujols by roughly a win and a half each season, with some change left over.

Had Pujols been on the Cardinals' roster, Peralta likely would have taken his talents elsewhere, and it's questionable whether the Cardinals would have felt as comfortable as they did in extending franchise icons Adam Wainwright and Yadier Molina with the contracts that they got. In 2014 and 2015, Molina made $15 million and Wainwright made $19.5 million, and both made sizeable contributions to the team. Maybe the Cardinals would have kept Waino and Yadi around, and some other contributor (Jon Jay?) would have been sent away. Then again, a more charitable read would be that Pujols's presence on the Cardinals' roster would have created a logjam at first base and would have forced the Cardinals to trade away either Craig or Adams for what at the time would have been considered a loss. Given that both men turned into pumpkins shortly thereafter, it might have actually been a blessing in disguise.

Verdict: In both 2014 and 2015, the Cardinals finished in first place in the Central, two games ahead of the Pittsburgh Pirates in each year. In our alternate universe with El Hombre still a Redbird, it's likely that Jhonny Peralta and at least one other contributor would have been lacking in the Cards' lineup, which would have been a difference of 2 or 3 wins. In 2014, three fewer wins would have knocked the Cardinals out of the playoffs, while in 2015, it would have knocked them into the second Wild Card spot. It's probably a good thing that Albert Pujols was no longer around. If the Cardinals cleared any value from their decision to let Albert walk (slowly) away, it was during these years.

2016-2018

St. Louis Cardinals 2019

And so we enter the modern era of Cardinal malaise. There's no glory (or high draft picks) in 80-something wins and no playoff appearances, but that's pretty much been the Cards for the last three seasons. Meanwhile, Albert Pujols made 25, then 26, then 27 million dollars (and on the whole functioned below replacement level) during the last three years with the Angels. His poor showing in the American League would have been exacerbated by the fact that the Cardinals, lacking the DH option, would either have to play him in the field—something that he stopped doing full time in 2016—or relegate him to a bench bat. Realistically, even the modest Jose Martinez would have been a better everyday option at first. Pujols might have already been politely asked to leave by this point.

On the banks of the Mississippi River though, the guys on whom the Cardinals seem to have spent the "Pujols money" haven't exactly covered themselves in glory. In 2016 and 2017, Jhonny Peralta suddenly forgot how to play baseball and turned in seasons of -0.3 and -0.5 WARP. Wainwright and Molina, once perennial All-Stars, turned into guys who are worthy of a roster spot, but nothing special. Still, that's better than a negative number, so the Cardinals were likely better off without Pujols than they would have been with him, but the Cardinals were still spending money on late career players in decline.

Verdict: Signing Albert Pujols probably would have meant that Adam Wainwright would have been slinging curveballs in San Diego by now. Even though the Cardinals were probably better for not having signed Pujols, they didn't make the playoffs with him, so it's not like things would be that much different.

2019 and beyond

This is the part where it becomes a team preview. It's tempting to look back on not signing Albert Pujols, seeing his dwindling WARP over the past half-decade, and figuring that the Cardinals now have "so much extra payroll flexibility" because they aren't responsible for paying him nearly $90 million over the next three years. Someone out there is tying the Cardinals trade for the last year of Paul Goldschmidt's contract to that fact right now. (He isn't blocked at first by Pujols!)

That's now how things work. An honest look at the Cardinals' payroll sheet tells a different story. Had the Cardinals signed Pujols and promised to pay him $28 and $29 million over the next two years for what everyone would have correctly predicted—even in 2011—would be "decline" years, it's very likely that they wouldn't have signed Yadier Molina to a contract that pays him $20 million in each of the next two years for what are likely to be Molina's "decline" years. (Yes, Molina gave the Cards 3.0 WARP last year, but 36-year-old catchers tend to be bad bets going forward.) There seems to be a piece of every team's payroll which is reserved for keeping around fan favorites and paying off the back ends of contracts given to star players signed five years earlier.

In a world where a win above replacement is allegedly worth $10 million, but the highest paid players in baseball are just now reaching toward the $40 million mark, we know that the real currency of the game at the high end of the free agent market is extra years on a contract. Partisans who lauded the Cardinals non-decision in the Winter of 2011 because it would allow the Cardinals to have more flexibility once 2019 rolled around are probably miffed to realize that the Cardinals just made a junior varsity version of the same—is mistake the correct word here?

In retrospect, the Cardinals probably did get the better of the decision not to sign Pujols to that ten-year deal that he wanted (and got from the Angels). Instead, they got two years of Carlos Beltrán who turned out to be Pujols's equal in value, then two years of good Jhonny Peralta and the ability to extend a couple of other guys, then two years of bad Jhonny Peralta, and finally, the back end of Yadier Molina's career. They got four years of pretty good performance, followed by a tailing off. The tailing off wasn't as severe as Pujols, nor was the cash outlay quite as much, and the net effect was a couple of wins of value—a phrase which by its construction under-sells how tremendously impactful "a couple wins of value" are—but it's funny to note that the arc of Pujols's replacements have tended to follow a somewhat less odious version of the path that contracts like Pujols's usually take.

If you want to look back on Cardinals management over the last decade and make some statement about their general abilities at navigating this whole baseball thing, the decision not to sign Albert Pujols was not a sign that they had somehow transcended the usual pratfalls of modern baseball free agency signings. They still did most of the same things that drive people crazy, but they had the good sense to do it a little bit at a time.

—*Russell Carleton is an author of Baseball Prospectus.*

Part 2: Player Analysis

Harrison Bader CF

Born: 06/03/94 Age: 25 Bats: R Throws: R
Height: 6'0" Weight: 195 Origin: Round 3, 2015 Draft (#100 overall)

YEAR	TEAM	LVL	AGE	PA	R	2B	3B	HR	RBI	BB	K	SB	CS	AVG/OBP/SLG
2016	MEM	AAA	22	161	22	7	1	3	17	11	38	2	3	.231/.298/.354
2016	SFD	AA	22	356	48	12	4	16	41	25	93	11	10	.283/.351/.497
2017	MEM	AAA	23	479	74	18	1	20	55	34	118	15	9	.283/.347/.469
2017	SLN	MLB	23	92	10	3	0	3	10	5	24	2	1	.235/.283/.376
2018	SLN	MLB	24	427	61	20	2	12	37	31	125	15	3	.264/.334/.422
2019	SLN	MLB	25	552	65	19	2	17	58	35	153	14	6	.231/.291/.378

Breakout: 18% Improve: 50% Collapse: 11% Attrition: 26% MLB: 89%
Comparables: Michael Taylor, Cameron Maybin, Peter Bourjos

If Starling Marte is a tall drink of water, physically, Bader is more like a shot of whiskey. Beyond that, however, there are striking similarities between them. Both have only average power, but stoked by their top-of-the-scale speed and aggressiveness, that plays up a bit, as doubles become triples, long singles become doubles, and singles become opportunities to steal second base. Both have strong arms in center field. When he's going well, Bader even shows good plate discipline, just as Marte does. The problem is, even more than Marte—more than almost anyone—Bader has contact problems. The only batters who fanned more often than Bader and had an ISO as low or lower than his were JaCoby Jones, Lewis Brinson, and Chris Davis. Unless and until he fixes that, he's going to be a suspect starting center fielder for a contender.

YEAR	TEAM	LVL	AGE	PA	DRC+	VORP	BABIP	BRR	FRAA	WARP
2016	MEM	AAA	22	161	75	2.5	.292	-0.1	CF(26): 1.5, LF(16): 0.7	0.0
2016	SFD	AA	22	356	130	29.5	.349	0.7	CF(77): 0.9, RF(4): -0.4	1.7
2017	MEM	AAA	23	479	118	40.8	.345	5.3	CF(111): 13.7, LF(3): -0.4	3.9
2017	SLN	MLB	23	92	82	1.3	.288	0.3	CF(20): 2.0, LF(7): -0.1	0.3
2018	SLN	MLB	24	427	90	24.7	.358	2.8	CF(74): 9.1, RF(38): 1.6	2.2
2019	SLN	MLB	25	552	84	12.8	.296	0.5	CF 9	2.0

Harrison Bader, continued

Batted Ball Distribution

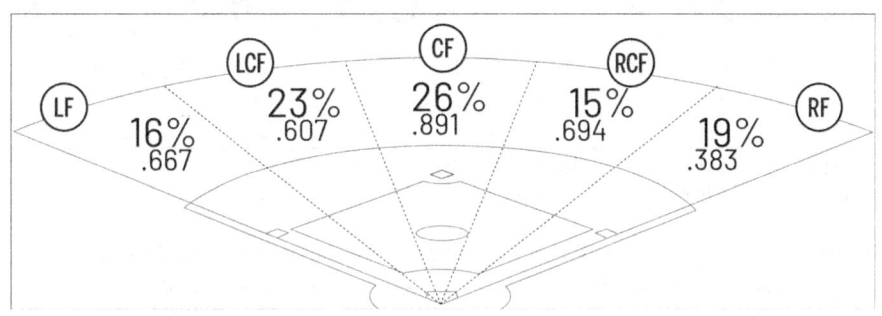

Strike Zone vs LHP

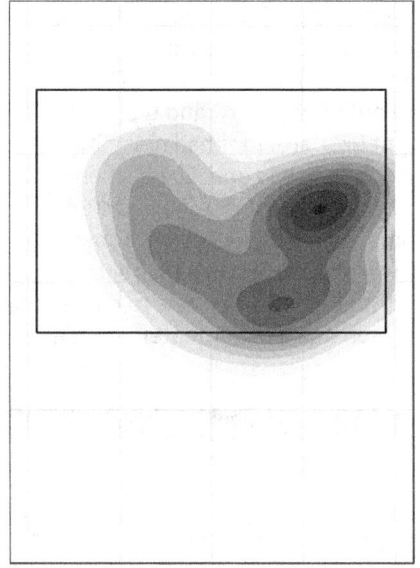

Strike Zone vs RHP

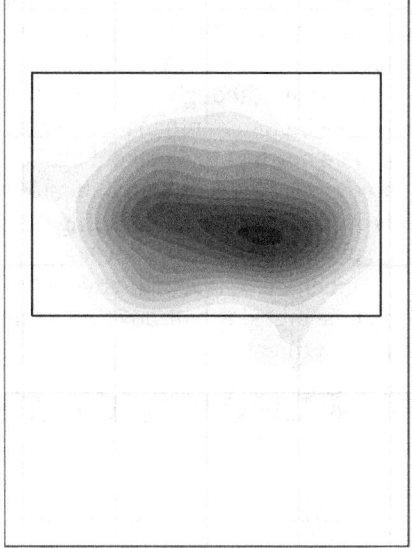

St. Louis Cardinals 2019

Matt Carpenter   3B

Born: 11/26/85   Age: 33   Bats: L   Throws: R
Height: 6'3"   Weight: 205   Origin: Round 13, 2009 Draft (#399 overall)

YEAR	TEAM	LVL	AGE	PA	R	2B	3B	HR	RBI	BB	K	SB	CS	AVG/OBP/SLG
2016	SLN	MLB	30	566	81	36	6	21	68	81	108	0	4	.271/.380/.505
2017	SLN	MLB	31	622	91	31	2	23	69	109	125	2	1	.241/.384/.451
2018	SLN	MLB	32	677	111	42	0	36	81	102	158	4	1	.257/.374/.523
2019	SLN	MLB	33	642	89	36	2	22	75	86	139	3	2	.253/.361/.449

Breakout: 0%   Improve: 22%   Collapse: 20%   Attrition: 13%   MLB: 97%
Comparables: Mark Teixeira, Paul Konerko, Nick Swisher

There are, perhaps, a half-dozen players who stand clear of the rest of the league in the simple and invaluable skill of generating high-value contact at a very high rate: J.D. Martinez, Khris Davis, Mookie Betts, Joey Gallo, Ryan Zimmerman, and now, Carpenter. The former average-over-power utility guy was on the cutting edge of the launch angle revolution, when he first got more aggressive, traded some contact for power, and lifted the ball more often. In 2018, he redoubled that tradeoff. If it was a science project, it was a successful experiment, because he ratcheted his ground-ball rate all the way down to the second-lowest in MLB, and he found an entirely new level of power. There's some evidence, though, that it was actually out of necessity, and that makes his outlook a bit dimmer than it otherwise might be. Carpenter had never had a whiff rate north of 10.6 percent against breaking pitches until 2018, when it soared to 15.7 percent. His whiff rate of 14.7 percent against offspeed stuff was only slightly less alarming. During the summer, when he locked onto some fastballs and laid waste to the league, that wasn't a huge concern, but by September, the league rediscovered his kryptonite and laid waste to him. In the age of the breaking ball, any fastball hitter, even one like Carpenter, is under imminent threat.

YEAR	TEAM	LVL	AGE	PA	DRC+	VORP	BABIP	BRR	FRAA	WARP
2016	SLN	MLB	30	566	126	45.7	.307	1.2	3B(54): -3.9, 1B(45): 0.1	2.9
2017	SLN	MLB	31	622	119	34.1	.274	-2.4	1B(120): 2.1, 3B(16): 0.9	2.7
2018	SLN	MLB	32	677	135	54.8	.291	-1.5	1B(95): -3.6, 3B(76): 4.8	4.6
2019	SLN	MLB	33	642	128	37.7	.298	-1.3	3B 4, 2B 0	4.0

Matt Carpenter, continued

Batted Ball Distribution

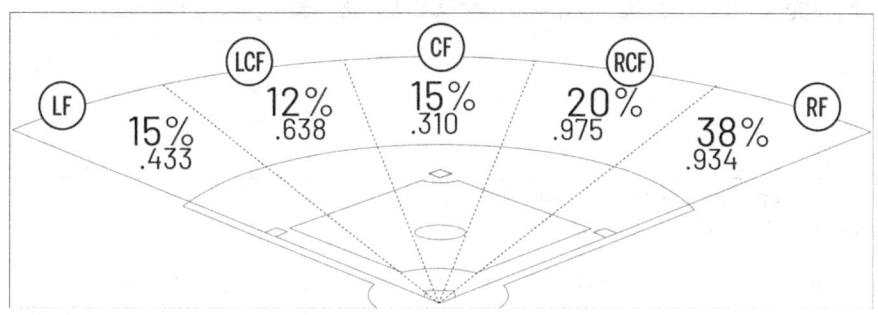

Strike Zone vs LHP   **Strike Zone vs RHP**

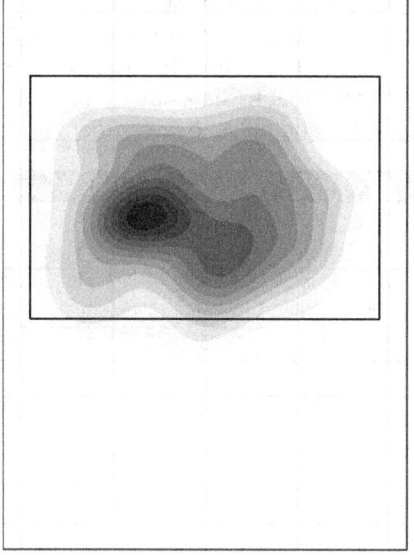

St. Louis Cardinals 2019

Paul DeJong SS
Born: 08/02/93 Age: 25 Bats: R Throws: R
Height: 6'1" Weight: 195 Origin: Round 4, 2015 Draft (#131 overall)

YEAR	TEAM	LVL	AGE	PA	R	2B	3B	HR	RBI	BB	K	SB	CS	AVG/OBP/SLG
2016	SFD	AA	22	552	62	29	2	22	73	40	144	3	2	.260/.324/.460
2017	MEM	AAA	23	190	27	9	0	13	34	9	46	0	2	.299/.339/.571
2017	SLN	MLB	23	443	55	26	1	25	65	21	124	1	0	.285/.325/.532
2018	SLN	MLB	24	490	68	25	1	19	68	36	123	1	1	.241/.313/.433
2019	SLN	MLB	25	581	66	27	2	23	77	41	148	1	1	.247/.309/.436

Breakout: 16% Improve: 59% Collapse: 14% Attrition: 12% MLB: 99%
Comparables: Trevor Story, Javier Baez, Ian Stewart

In every important way, 2018 was a big step forward for DeJong. He hit the ball harder, and regularly put it in the air. He dialed back his aggressiveness early in counts and drew more walks. He used the opposite field better, and made a much-needed adjustment against breaking balls from fellow right-handers, helping him cut down his strikeout rate. After living as an infield nomad on his way up the ladder, he settled in as the Cardinals' everyday shortstop and improved as a defender there. His rookie numbers were fluky, but given his age and rapid maturation, his true talent level seems to be progressing toward matching them. Chalk him up as another huge win for the St. Louis amateur scouting and player development units.

YEAR	TEAM	LVL	AGE	PA	DRC+	VORP	BABIP	BRR	FRAA	WARP
2016	SFD	AA	22	552	117	31.1	.318	-1.8	3B(112): -4.3, SS(11): 0.9	1.1
2017	MEM	AAA	23	190	130	18.0	.336	-1.0	SS(39): -3.8, 2B(5): 0.4	0.8
2017	SLN	MLB	23	443	115	32.4	.349	-3.9	SS(86): -0.3, 2B(20): -0.7	2.3
2018	SLN	MLB	24	490	101	34.8	.288	3.1	SS(114): 0.3	2.7
2019	SLN	MLB	25	581	106	27.3	.297	-1.1	SS -1	2.4

Paul DeJong, continued

Batted Ball Distribution

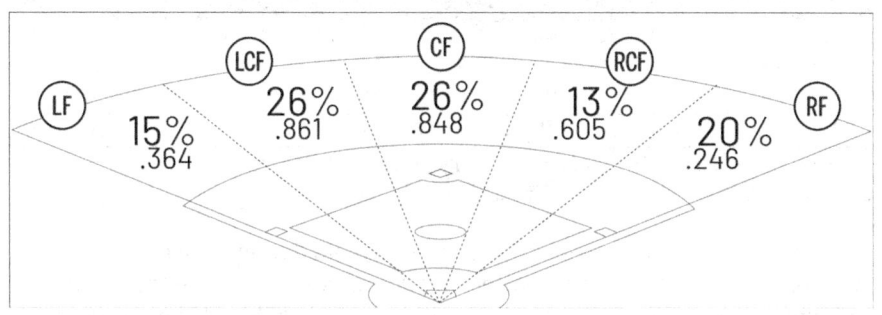

Strike Zone vs LHP   **Strike Zone vs RHP**

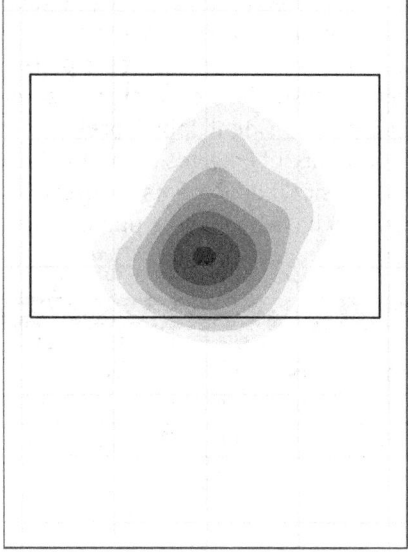

St. Louis Cardinals 2019

Dexter Fowler   OF

Born: 03/22/86   Age: 33   Bats: B   Throws: R
Height: 6'5"   Weight: 195   Origin: Round 14, 2004 Draft (#410 overall)

YEAR	TEAM	LVL	AGE	PA	R	2B	3B	HR	RBI	BB	K	SB	CS	AVG/OBP/SLG
2016	CHN	MLB	30	551	84	25	7	13	48	79	124	13	4	.276/.393/.447
2017	SLN	MLB	31	491	68	22	9	18	64	63	101	7	3	.264/.363/.488
2018	SLN	MLB	32	334	40	10	0	8	31	38	75	5	2	.180/.278/.298
2019	SLN	MLB	33	273	31	12	2	7	30	29	61	5	2	.247/.333/.402

Breakout: 2%   Improve: 24%   Collapse: 18%   Attrition: 9%   MLB: 94%
Comparables: Matt Joyce, Trot Nixon, Jim King

The Cardinals' decision to move Fowler to right field during the winter of 2017-18 was fraught with risk. Fowler's weaknesses as a center fielder (a lack of confidence in charging ground-ball hits, a weak arm) could only be exacerbated by that change. Asking him to learn new angles and still cover an outfield spot didn't reduce the risk of injury to his lanky, sometimes-fragile frame, the way a transition to first base might have. Most importantly, however, the move sent a clear message to Fowler: one year into a five-year deal, he was being demoted and deprioritized. He also lost his place at the top of the batting order, forcing him to alter his approach at the plate. He tried to do so; he failed. Then, amid a painful season for a player with a sterling reputation for clubhouse citizenship, Cardinals president John Mozeliak piled on, wielding harsh and insensitive remarks about Fowler's effort and focus. Fowler was unable to make the mental and physical adjustments necessary to succeed, but few players in recent memory have been more unfairly mistreated and misunderstood by their own team.

YEAR	TEAM	LVL	AGE	PA	DRC+	VORP	BABIP	BRR	FRAA	WARP
2016	CHN	MLB	30	551	111	47.1	.350	1.1	CF(121): -11.4	1.6
2017	SLN	MLB	31	491	118	36.9	.305	1.4	CF(109): -10.1	2.0
2018	SLN	MLB	32	334	77	-1.6	.210	2.0	RF(75): -4.3	-0.4
2019	SLN	MLB	33	273	104	9.9	.298	0.2	RF -2	0.7

Dexter Fowler, continued

Batted Ball Distribution

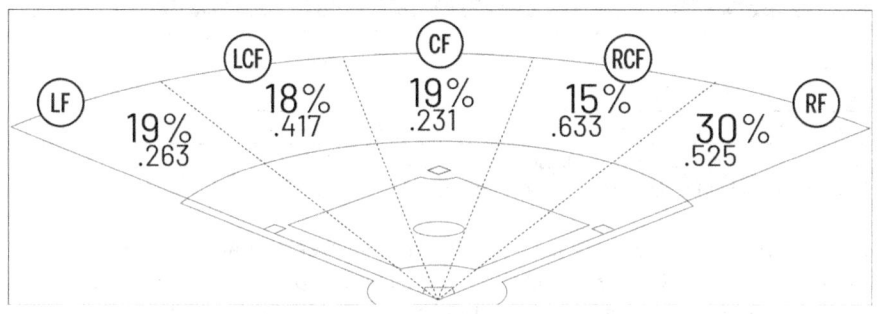

Strike Zone vs LHP   **Strike Zone vs RHP**

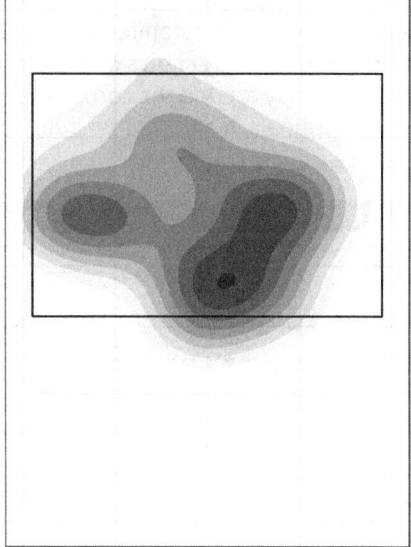

Paul Goldschmidt 1B

Born: 09/10/87 Age: 31 Bats: R Throws: R
Height: 6'3" Weight: 225 Origin: Round 8, 2009 Draft (#246 overall)

YEAR	TEAM	LVL	AGE	PA	R	2B	3B	HR	RBI	BB	K	SB	CS	AVG/OBP/SLG
2016	ARI	MLB	28	705	106	33	3	24	95	110	150	32	5	.297/.411/.489
2017	ARI	MLB	29	665	117	34	3	36	120	94	147	18	5	.297/.404/.563
2018	ARI	MLB	30	690	95	35	5	33	83	90	173	7	4	.290/.389/.533
2019	SLN	MLB	31	653	92	29	3	24	87	97	154	16	4	.275/.388/.471

Breakout: 2% Improve: 29% Collapse: 17% Attrition: 5% MLB: 99%
Comparables: Lance Berkman, Mark Teixeira, Jason Giambi

It was a late, drizzly, cold night in Smallville. The streets of America were quiet for a change when Clark Kent and Lois Lane curled up on the couch under a warm, fuzzy blanket. Not knowing what to do with a little down time, Lois looked to Kent and asked, "Netflix and chill?" Clark responded with a confused look, but after some searching on Urban Dictionary and roughly nine months of incubation, Paul Goldschmidt was born. Thirty years later, Goldschmidt continues to impose justice on opposing pitching. An early season run-in with some mysterious kryptonite gave way to four splendid months of superhero-like production as Goldy shows no signs of truly slowing down. With free agency and a huge payday around the corner, the rebuilding Diamondbacks sent Superman to the Cardinals in a December blockbuster, closing the book on a spectacular eight-season run in Arizona.

YEAR	TEAM	LVL	AGE	PA	DRC+	VORP	BABIP	BRR	FRAA	WARP
2016	ARI	MLB	28	705	129	45.3	.358	1.5	1B(157): 16.1	5.2
2017	ARI	MLB	29	665	140	58.0	.343	3.7	1B(151): 5.7	5.1
2018	ARI	MLB	30	690	136	54.6	.359	-1.3	1B(155): 1.7	4.1
2019	SLN	MLB	31	653	141	46.6	.337	0.7	1B 6	5.4

Paul Goldschmidt, continued

Batted Ball Distribution

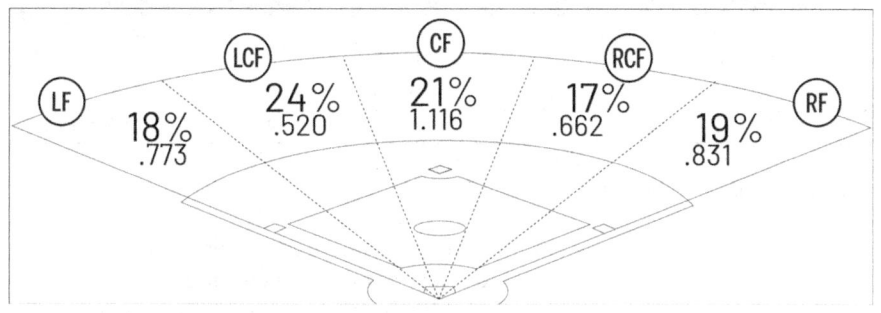

Strike Zone vs LHP

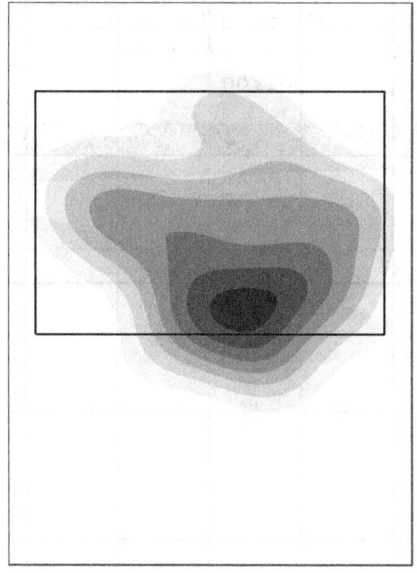

Strike Zone vs RHP

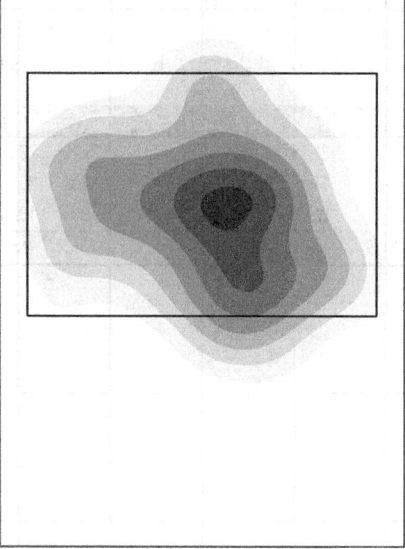

Jedd Gyorko INF

Born: 09/23/88   Age: 30   Bats: R   Throws: R
Height: 5'10"   Weight: 215   Origin: Round 2, 2010 Draft (#59 overall)

YEAR	TEAM	LVL	AGE	PA	R	2B	3B	HR	RBI	BB	K	SB	CS	AVG/OBP/SLG
2016	SLN	MLB	27	438	58	9	1	30	59	37	96	0	0	.243/.306/.495
2017	SLN	MLB	28	481	52	21	2	20	67	47	105	6	2	.272/.341/.472
2018	SLN	MLB	29	402	49	19	1	11	47	44	77	2	0	.262/.346/.416
2019	SLN	MLB	30	230	26	10	1	8	29	22	48	1	0	.255/.330/.431

Breakout: 0%   Improve: 32%   Collapse: 20%   Attrition: 6%   MLB: 91%
Comparables: Trevor Plouffe, Hank Blalock, Mark Teahen

For the third time in three years with the Cardinals, Gyorko set a new career mark in on-base percentage, struck out less often than ever, and walked more than ever. He's not the power hitter his bizarre 2016 suggested he was, but in every other way, he's only getting better. Despite being even slower than his frame suggests, he's also used sure hands and good footwork to deliver value as a fine defender at second or third base. It all figures to go slowly downhill as he enters his thirties, but also, who thought three years ago we'd be worrying about Jedd Gyoko's thirties? As it turns out, he's given himself a surprisingly wide base of skills on which to lean as that process goes on.

YEAR	TEAM	LVL	AGE	PA	DRC+	VORP	BABIP	BRR	FRAA	WARP
2016	SLN	MLB	27	438	121	28.3	.244	0.6	2B(46): 5.1, 3B(39): -1.6	3.2
2017	SLN	MLB	28	481	113	28.4	.312	-0.4	3B(109): 10.7, 1B(10): 0.5	3.7
2018	SLN	MLB	29	402	109	18.0	.303	-1.2	3B(96): -4.8, 2B(17): 0.1	1.3
2019	SLN	MLB	30	230	106	8.6	.288	-0.2	3B 0, 2B 1	1.0

Jedd Gyorko, continued

Batted Ball Distribution

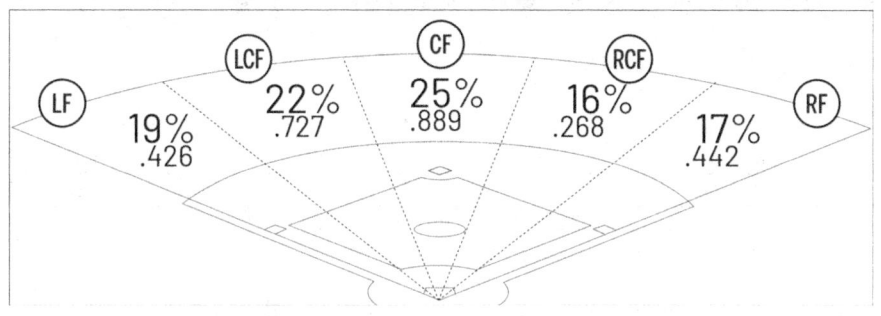

Strike Zone vs LHP

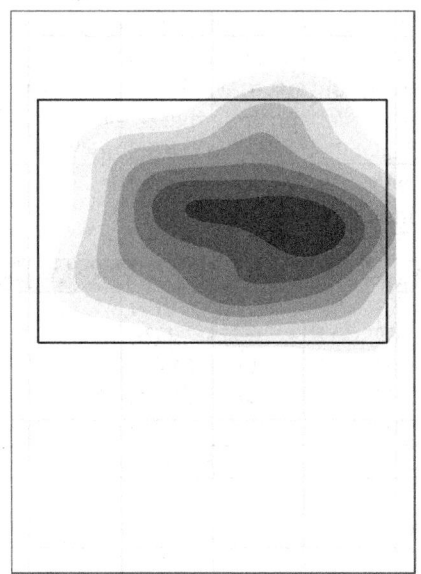

Strike Zone vs RHP

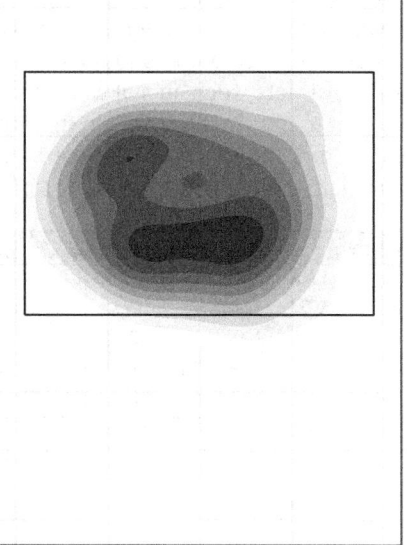

St. Louis Cardinals 2019

Jose Martinez 1B
Born: 07/25/88   Age: 30   Bats: R   Throws: R
Height: 6'6"   Weight: 215   Origin: International Free Agent, 2006

YEAR	TEAM	LVL	AGE	PA	R	2B	3B	HR	RBI	BB	K	SB	CS	AVG/OBP/SLG
2016	OMA	AAA	27	160	18	10	0	3	18	14	24	2	0	.298/.356/.433
2016	MEM	AAA	27	329	34	18	1	8	42	25	50	9	1	.269/.326/.415
2016	SLN	MLB	27	18	4	1	0	0	1	2	1	0	0	.438/.500/.500
2017	SLN	MLB	28	307	47	13	1	14	46	32	60	4	0	.309/.379/.518
2018	SLN	MLB	29	590	64	30	0	17	83	49	104	0	3	.305/.364/.457
2019	SLN	MLB	30	450	50	20	1	13	53	38	87	3	1	.264/.330/.415

Breakout: 4%   Improve: 41%   Collapse: 16%   Attrition: 12%   MLB: 85%
Comparables: Nolan Reimold, Jesus Guzman, Ryan Garko

Though not as tall or as thick and muscular as Aaron Judge or Giancarlo Stanton, Martinez manages the same aesthetic that Dave Winfield did during his heyday. He entirely fills up the right-handed batter's box. He seems too big to imagine getting him out. Alas, that's where any comparison to Winfield stops cold. Martinez is a fine hitter, using the whole field and generating average-plus power, but he's overly aggressive early in counts, so he doesn't get on base the way such a gifted batter should. In unforgiving contrast to Winfield, he's also a terrible athlete, such an awkward defender at every position that to even attempt to play regularly afield threatens his ability to stay in the lineup. You want more power or a more discerning eye from a DH, and if you're the Cardinals, an actual DH position to play him in.

YEAR	TEAM	LVL	AGE	PA	DRC+	VORP	BABIP	BRR	FRAA	WARP
2016	OMA	AAA	27	160	107	9.6	.331	1.1	1B(20): -1.6, LF(12): -0.8	0.0
2016	MEM	AAA	27	329	110	3.4	.299	-1.2	LF(30): -0.2, RF(29): 0.5	0.2
2016	SLN	MLB	27	18	101	2.6	.467	0.4	LF(4): 0.3, 1B(1): 0.0	0.1
2017	SLN	MLB	28	307	128	25.2	.350	0.1	1B(33): 0.0, LF(24): -2.8	1.4
2018	SLN	MLB	29	590	119	29.7	.351	-3.6	1B(84): -10.4, RF(46): 0.2	0.9
2019	SLN	MLB	30	450	107	16.3	.305	-0.8	RF -4, 1B -1	1.1

Jose Martinez, continued

Batted Ball Distribution

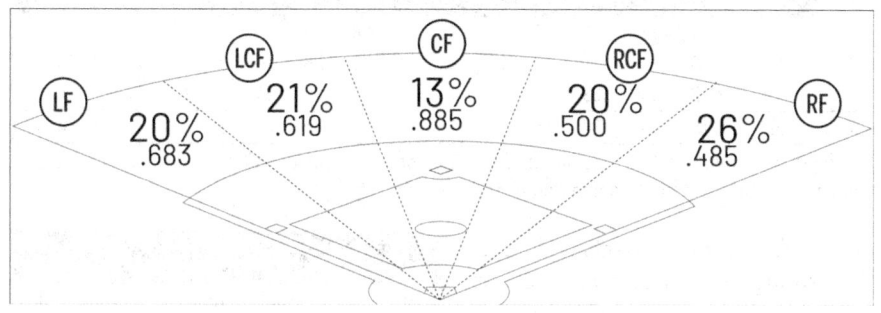

Strike Zone vs LHP

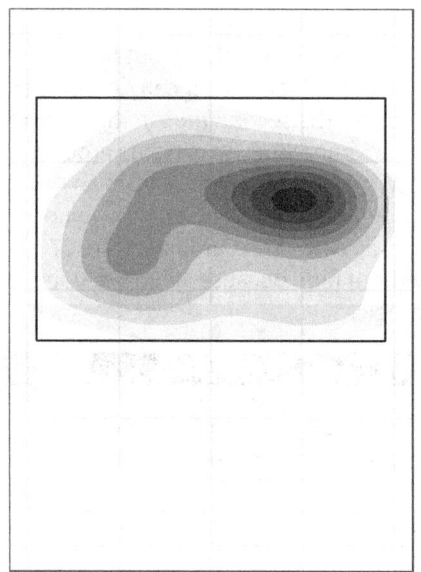

Strike Zone vs RHP

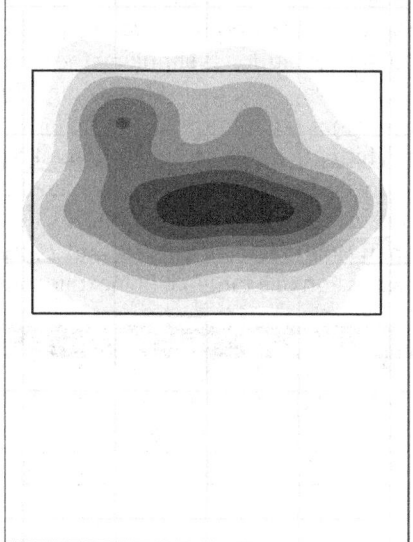

Yadier Molina C

Born: 07/13/82   Age: 36   Bats: R   Throws: R
Height: 5'11"   Weight: 205   Origin: Round 4, 2000 Draft (#113 overall)

YEAR	TEAM	LVL	AGE	PA	R	2B	3B	HR	RBI	BB	K	SB	CS	AVG/OBP/SLG
2016	SLN	MLB	33	581	56	38	1	8	58	39	63	3	2	.307/.360/.427
2017	SLN	MLB	34	543	60	27	1	18	82	28	74	9	4	.273/.312/.439
2018	SLN	MLB	35	503	55	20	0	20	74	29	66	4	3	.261/.314/.436
2019	SLN	MLB	36	534	66	28	1	14	55	35	77	5	3	.273/.326/.420

Breakout: 1%   Improve: 24%   Collapse: 13%   Attrition: 24%   MLB: 68%
Comparables: Hank Severeid, Ramon Hernandez, Mike Lieberthal

YEAR	TEAM	P. COUNT	FRM RUNS	BLK RUNS	THRW RUNS	TOT RUNS
2016	SLN	19667	10.4	1.6	-0.9	10.7
2017	SLN	18649	6.4	0.2	2.2	9.3
2018	SLN	17163	2.3	1.2	0.1	3.5
2019	SLN	17564	2.5	0.9	-0.3	3.2

An invisible string connects Molina to the beating heart of baseball itself. As the game changes, Molina's game changes. As he ages and the accretion of innings behind the plate diminishes him, the game comes back to him a bit. Molina was still an average-plus framer in 2018 (though a worse one than he'd ever been before), but the league's evolution is shrinking the value any individual catcher can deliver that way anyway. He was just an average thrower, for the second time in three years, but no one steals bases anymore anyway. He's gone from an extreme ground-ball hitter to one who hits fly balls at a pretty high rate. He's gone from an opposite-field singles hitter to a dead-pull, 20-homer guy, but it's hard to notice because everyone's already hitting that way anyway. The Cardinals were 67-53 when Molina started in 2018, and 21-21 without him, because Molina remains in possession of a tangible (if inexplicable) magic.

YEAR	TEAM	LVL	AGE	PA	DRC+	VORP	BABIP	BRR	FRAA	WARP
2016	SLN	MLB	33	581	107	29.0	.335	-7.7	C(146): 11.7, 1B(2): 0.0	3.8
2017	SLN	MLB	34	543	102	21.0	.285	-4.5	C(133): 6.0, 1B(1): 0.0	3.0
2018	SLN	MLB	35	503	111	27.7	.264	-2.3	C(121): 1.4, 1B(5): 0.0	3.1
2019	SLN	MLB	36	534	107	25.5	.297	-0.8	C -1	2.6

Yadier Molina, continued

Batted Ball Distribution

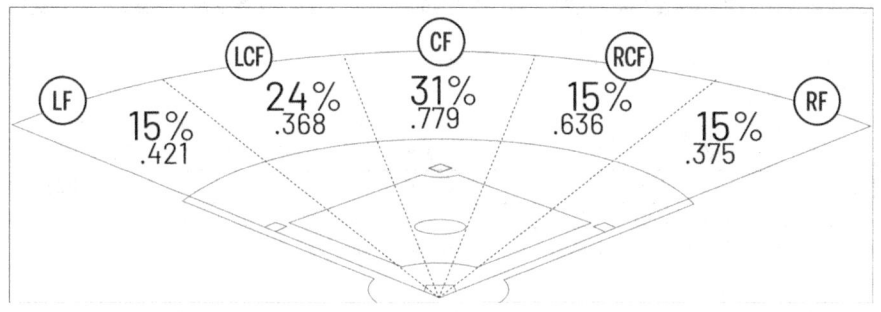

Strike Zone vs LHP

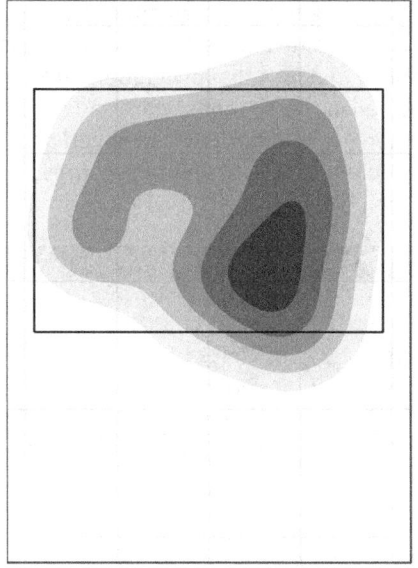

Strike Zone vs RHP

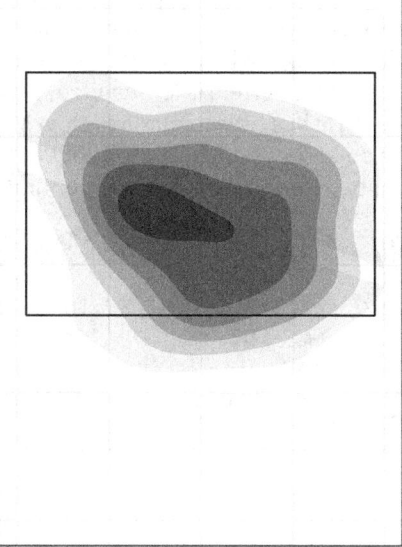

St. Louis Cardinals 2019

Yairo Munoz UT
Born: 01/23/95   Age: 24   Bats: R   Throws: R
Height: 6'1"   Weight: 201   Origin: International Free Agent, 2012

YEAR	TEAM	LVL	AGE	PA	R	2B	3B	HR	RBI	BB	K	SB	CS	AVG/OBP/SLG
2016	MID	AA	21	414	44	16	3	9	39	23	76	6	7	.240/.286/.367
2017	MID	AA	22	207	35	17	3	6	26	10	35	12	1	.316/.348/.532
2017	NAS	AAA	22	272	30	9	1	7	42	11	46	10	4	.289/.316/.414
2018	MEM	AAA	23	100	11	3	1	3	13	5	18	1	0	.287/.330/.436
2018	SLN	MLB	23	329	39	16	0	8	42	30	71	5	6	.276/.350/.413
2019	SLN	MLB	24	158	18	5	1	4	16	12	33	3	2	.245/.310/.378

Breakout: 13%   Improve: 55%   Collapse: 9%   Attrition: 23%   MLB: 87%
Comparables: Josh Rutledge, Enrique Hernandez, Stephen Drew

The thickset Munoz is stretched a bit thin at shortstop these days, which is unfortunate. His bat doesn't play all that well at third base, where teams want more power, or at second, where teams increasingly feel they can skate a bit defensively in order to squeeze out some extra offense at the position. If he'd arrived before DeJong, perhaps he could have disguised himself among the stockier generation of Cardinals shortstops that came before, but alas. Munoz is a free-swinger whose approach almost exactly matches that of Odubel Herrera, except that Herrera is left-handed, gets the ball in the air more often, and runs faster. He has time to mature into a 20-homer guy, and both the bat speed and the build suggest it's possible, but unless and until that possibility becomes a reality, he's no more than a suboptimal bench bat.

YEAR	TEAM	LVL	AGE	PA	DRC+	VORP	BABIP	BRR	FRAA	WARP
2016	MID	AA	21	414	76	1.1	.278	-1.0	SS(41): 0.9, 2B(27): 0.5	-0.3
2017	MID	AA	22	207	117	18.2	.355	3.2	SS(22): -1.1, 3B(21): -0.3	0.8
2017	NAS	AAA	22	272	92	7.8	.324	-2.9	SS(24): 2.4, CF(19): -1.9	0.4
2018	MEM	AAA	23	100	104	7.2	.329	0.3	SS(13): 0.2, LF(4): -0.5	0.2
2018	SLN	MLB	23	329	101	16.9	.338	-2.5	SS(40): -5.4, 2B(26): -0.8	0.2
2019	SLN	MLB	24	158	95	4.3	.290	-0.1	SS 0, 2B 0	0.4

Yairo Munoz, continued

Batted Ball Distribution

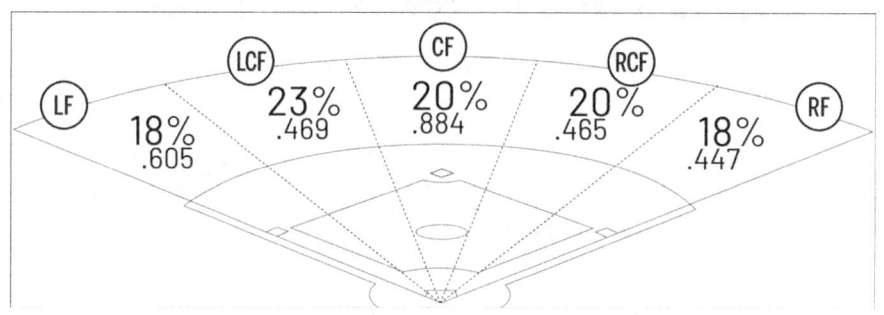

Strike Zone vs LHP   Strike Zone vs RHP

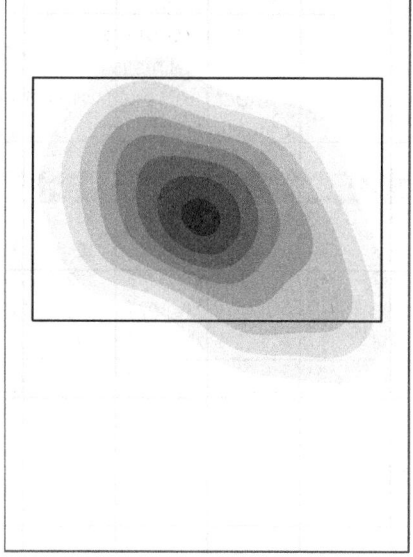

St. Louis Cardinals 2019

Tyler O'Neill RF
Born: 06/22/95   Age: 24   Bats: R   Throws: R
Height: 5'11"   Weight: 210   Origin: Round 3, 2013 Draft (#85 overall)

YEAR	TEAM	LVL	AGE	PA	R	2B	3B	HR	RBI	BB	K	SB	CS	AVG/OBP/SLG
2016	WTN	AA	21	575	68	26	4	24	102	62	150	12	2	.293/.374/.508
2017	TAC	AAA	22	396	54	21	2	19	56	44	108	9	2	.244/.328/.479
2017	MEM	AAA	22	161	23	5	1	12	39	10	43	5	0	.253/.304/.548
2018	MEM	AAA	23	273	61	9	2	26	63	29	68	3	1	.311/.385/.693
2018	SLN	MLB	23	142	29	5	0	9	23	7	57	2	0	.254/.303/.500
2019	SLN	MLB	24	199	26	7	1	11	30	16	62	2	0	.233/.300/.467

Breakout: 14%   Improve: 47%   Collapse: 16%   Attrition: 29%   MLB: 79%
Comparables: Paul Goldschmidt, George Springer, Christin Stewart

There's absolutely nothing subtle about O'Neill, and the only polished thing about him is his physique. A very good athlete, he's a poor outfielder, still trying to get the knack of reading balls off the bat and tracking them in the air. His power is as impressive as his pecs and his stats suggest, but his failure to make contact against big-league pitching was historic—'no batter has ever made contact on a lower percentage of swings in a season where they saw 500 or more pitches' historic. This is the era of the strikeout, but O'Neill still has to make more contact (and get more refined in other areas, too) in order to rise above the Incaviglia level of baseball lore.

YEAR	TEAM	LVL	AGE	PA	DRC+	VORP	BABIP	BRR	FRAA	WARP
2016	WTN	AA	21	575	144	47.4	.364	-0.8	RF(108): -4.0, LF(5): -0.3	2.1
2017	TAC	AAA	22	396	104	19.3	.295	0.3	LF(67): -1.8, RF(17): -0.9	0.4
2017	MEM	AAA	22	161	102	7.0	.266	-0.6	RF(18): 1.0, LF(10): -0.3	0.2
2018	MEM	AAA	23	273	163	40.8	.324	1.0	LF(33): -1.3, RF(21): 7.8	2.9
2018	SLN	MLB	23	142	90	11.5	.364	2.2	RF(24): 0.7, LF(16): 1.1	0.5
2019	SLN	MLB	24	199	113	9.6	.286	0.1	LF -1, RF 0	0.9

Tyler O'Neill, continued

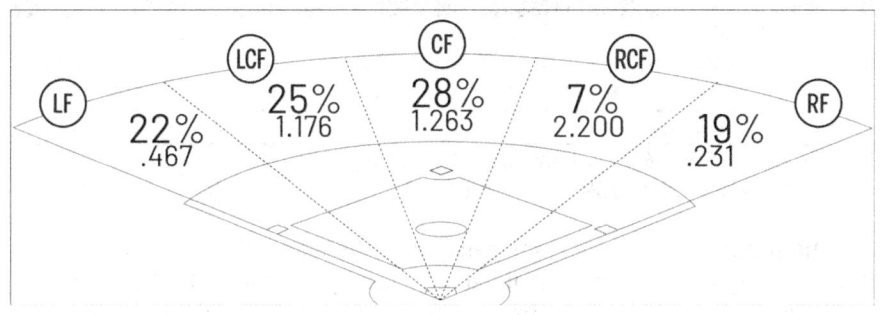

Marcell Ozuna LF

Born: 11/12/90 Age: 28 Bats: R Throws: R
Height: 6'1" Weight: 225 Origin: International Free Agent, 2008

YEAR	TEAM	LVL	AGE	PA	R	2B	3B	HR	RBI	BB	K	SB	CS	AVG/OBP/SLG
2016	MIA	MLB	25	608	75	23	6	23	76	43	115	0	3	.266/.321/.452
2017	MIA	MLB	26	679	93	30	2	37	124	64	144	1	3	.312/.376/.548
2018	SLN	MLB	27	628	69	16	2	23	88	38	110	3	0	.280/.325/.433
2019	SLN	MLB	28	565	67	23	2	22	75	45	108	2	1	.272/.333/.453

Breakout: 2% Improve: 36% Collapse: 18% Attrition: 6% MLB: 96%
Comparables: Del Ennis, George Bell, Wes Covington

The sharp statistical disparity between Ozuna's breakout 2017 and his disappointing 2018 can't be explained away just by pointing out the lingering and enigmatic shoulder injury that hampered him, nor by good luck in the former campaign and bad luck in the latter one. All of those things contributed to the downturn, though. Ozuna hit 87 balls hard to the left side in 2017, and slugged 1.506 on them. In 2018, he hit 88 such balls in fewer total plate appearances—but slugged 1.034. His average launch angle on those hits dropped by about six degrees. In protecting his shoulder, he got less aggressive about going out and contacting the ball early. He leveled out his swing, to transfer energy into his front side sooner. He also made minor changes in approach that sapped some of his aggressiveness, leading to more contact but less power. Heading into his late 20s and with no clear answers about the shoulder, Ozuna shouldn't be expected to turn right back into an elite slugger, and heading into a contract year, he can't be fully trusted to bring his approach back into equilibrium.

YEAR	TEAM	LVL	AGE	PA	DRC+	VORP	BABIP	BRR	FRAA	WARP
2016	MIA	MLB	25	608	112	39.5	.296	1.6	CF(123): -7.2, LF(11): -1.4	2.5
2017	MIA	MLB	26	679	134	55.5	.355	-3.5	LF(152): 4.9, CF(3): 0.0	4.8
2018	SLN	MLB	27	628	109	30.4	.309	2.6	LF(147): -2.2	2.4
2019	SLN	MLB	28	565	116	28.6	.307	-1.0	LF -1	2.5

Marcell Ozuna, continued

Batted Ball Distribution

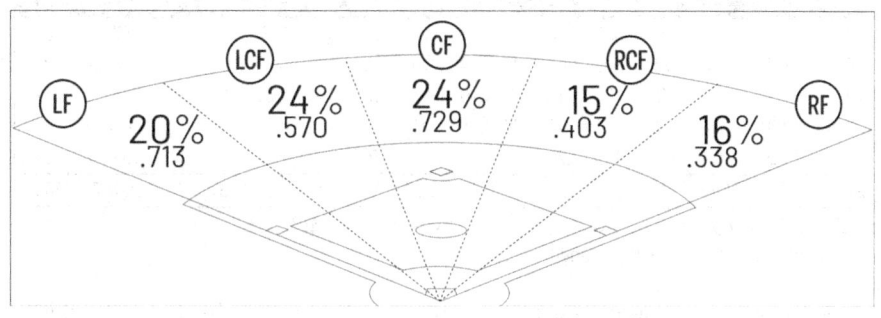

Strike Zone vs LHP   **Strike Zone vs RHP**

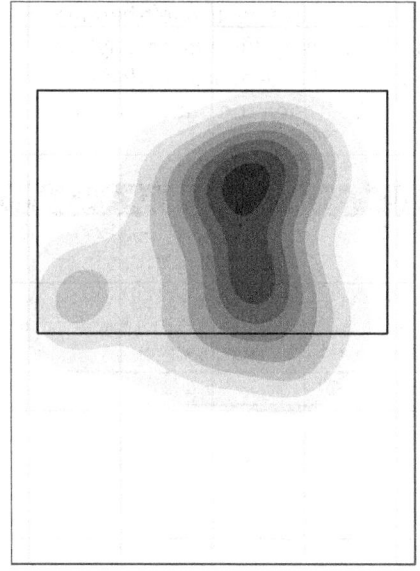 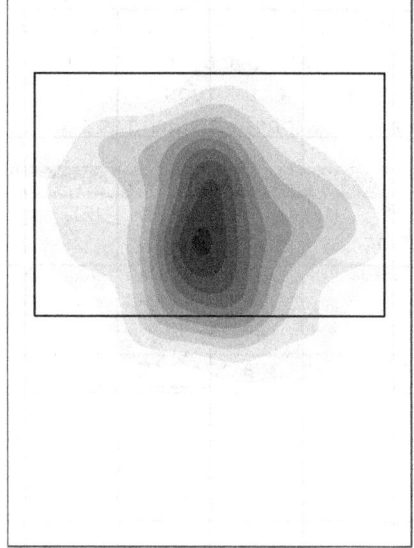

Drew Robinson UT

Born: 04/20/92 Age: 27 Bats: L Throws: R
Height: 6'1" Weight: 200 Origin: Round 4, 2010 Draft (#136 overall)

YEAR	TEAM	LVL	AGE	PA	R	2B	3B	HR	RBI	BB	K	SB	CS	AVG/OBP/SLG
2016	ROU	AAA	24	539	76	24	10	20	67	66	148	17	5	.257/.350/.480
2017	ROU	AAA	25	309	48	19	4	11	40	42	74	7	4	.268/.369/.494
2017	TEX	MLB	25	121	11	5	0	6	13	14	42	0	2	.224/.314/.439
2018	ROU	AAA	26	241	40	16	5	10	28	27	84	5	6	.303/.379/.569
2018	TEX	MLB	26	125	20	3	0	3	9	16	57	2	1	.183/.288/.294
2019	SLN	MLB	27	172	22	7	1	6	18	17	55	3	2	.211/.292/.388

Breakout: 5% Improve: 23% Collapse: 14% Attrition: 19% MLB: 56%
Comparables: Keon Broxton, Brandon Allen, Corey Brown

Is there a way to call someone a Quadruple-A player and not be mean about it? Let's try. Robinson is a very good minor-league player whose defense and ability to keep the clubhouse and bench loose are absolutely ready to make him a big-league player. Unfortunately, his bat has thus far not been able to catch up. If you're looking for an upside, his numbers in the majors against left-handed pitching are vastly better than expected. Unfortunately, his numbers against right-handers have been significantly worse than the team has needed from him. He's older than you think (27 in April), so he'll soon run out of shots to carve out a long-term niche as a utility player.

YEAR	TEAM	LVL	AGE	PA	DRC+	VORP	BABIP	BRR	FRAA	WARP
2016	ROU	AAA	24	539	120	45.5	.332	3.5	RF(38): 5.1, 2B(27): -1.2	2.3
2017	ROU	AAA	25	309	123	23.0	.331	0.8	2B(39): -2.6, CF(15): -0.5	1.3
2017	TEX	MLB	25	121	78	0.8	.305	-0.7	3B(20): -0.7, LF(15): -1.1	-0.1
2018	ROU	AAA	26	241	133	25.1	.454	-2.5	CF(40): 5.3, LF(5): 1.4	1.8
2018	TEX	MLB	26	125	47	-1.1	.347	1.2	CF(22): 0.8, LF(9): -0.8	-0.3
2019	SLN	MLB	27	172	92	4.2	.288	-0.1	2B 0, RF 0	0.4

Drew Robinson, continued

Batted Ball Distribution

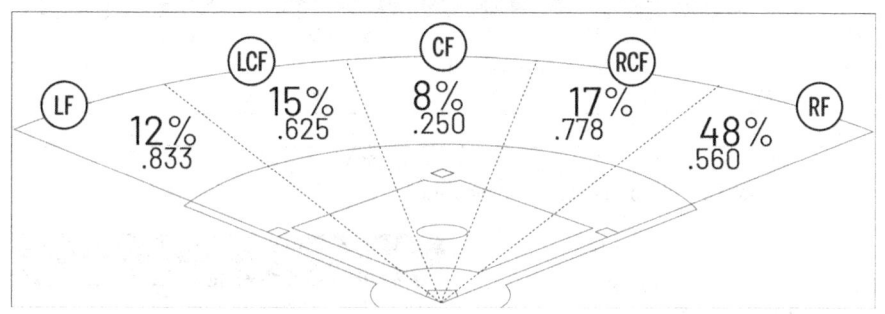

Strike Zone vs LHP   Strike Zone vs RHP

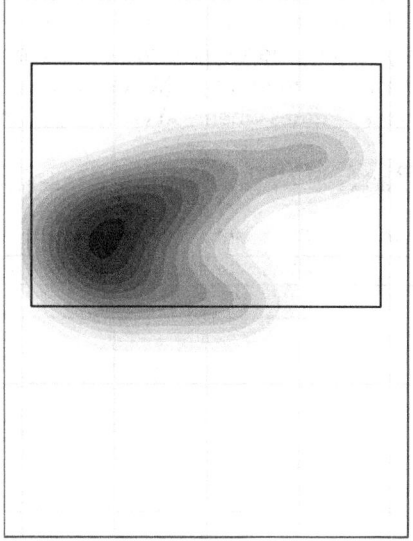

Matt Wieters C

Born: 05/21/86 Age: 33 Bats: B Throws: R
Height: 6'5" Weight: 235 Origin: Round 1, 2007 Draft (#5 overall)

YEAR	TEAM	LVL	AGE	PA	R	2B	3B	HR	RBI	BB	K	SB	CS	AVG/OBP/SLG
2016	BAL	MLB	30	464	48	17	1	17	66	32	85	1	0	.243/.302/.409
2017	WAS	MLB	31	465	43	20	0	10	52	38	94	1	0	.225/.288/.344
2018	WAS	MLB	32	271	24	8	0	8	30	30	45	0	1	.238/.330/.374
2019	SLN	MLB	33	129	13	6	0	3	13	10	24	0	0	.239/.302/.368

Breakout: 2% Improve: 35% Collapse: 12% Attrition: 19% MLB: 91%
Comparables: Rod Barajas, A.J. Pierzynski, Jimmie Wilson

Wieters, like waiters, can be most noticeable in absentia. Bringing ribeyes? Not necessary, just keep showing up and presenting the dishes well enough. His performance was just a touch over replacement level when he was on the field in 2018, but the real issue came when oblique and hamstring injuries left the Nationals out to dry for large portions of what was supposed to be a contending year. It didn't even really matter that he was being paid somewhat gratuitously. It was just one of those times when you want to pay the tab and move on with your life.

YEAR	TEAM	P. COUNT	FRM RUNS	BLK RUNS	THRW RUNS	TOT RUNS
2016	BAL	16454	0.7	1.0	1.9	4.3
2017	WAS	16476	-11.2	1.5	-0.7	-11.0
2018	WAS	9086	-3.7	1.1	0.3	-2.3
2019	SLN	4698	-2.6	0.4	0.0	-2.2

YEAR	TEAM	LVL	AGE	PA	DRC+	VORP	BABIP	BRR	FRAA	WARP
2016	BAL	MLB	30	464	98	12.0	.265	-1.4	C(117): 4.0	2.4
2017	WAS	MLB	31	465	74	1.9	.264	-1.7	C(118): -10.4	-0.4
2018	WAS	MLB	32	271	101	7.8	.261	-0.8	C(73): -4.0	0.9
2019	SLN	MLB	33	129	85	3.5	.275	-0.2	C -3	0.0

Matt Wieters, continued

Batted Ball Distribution

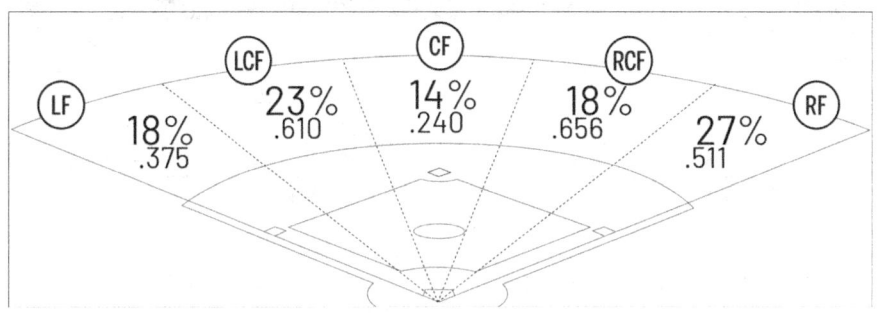

Strike Zone vs LHP   Strike Zone vs RHP

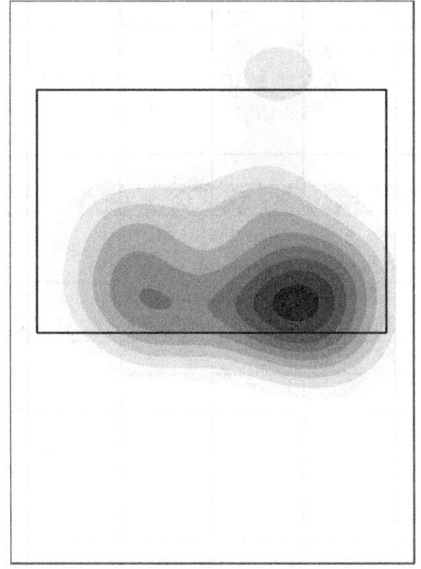
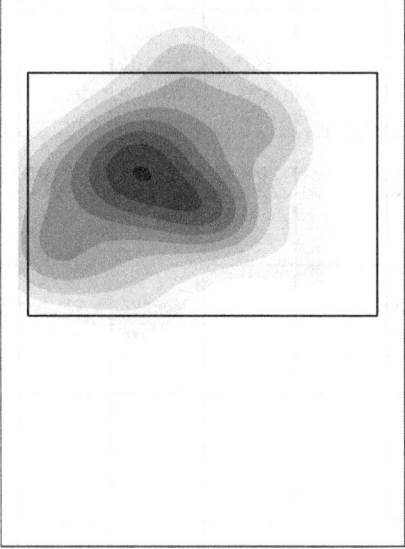

Kolten Wong 2B

Born: 10/10/90 Age: 28 Bats: L Throws: R
Height: 5'9" Weight: 185 Origin: Round 1, 2011 Draft (#22 overall)

YEAR	TEAM	LVL	AGE	PA	R	2B	3B	HR	RBI	BB	K	SB	CS	AVG/OBP/SLG
2016	MEM	AAA	25	34	10	0	1	4	11	4	6	1	0	.429/.529/.929
2016	SLN	MLB	25	361	39	7	7	5	23	34	52	7	0	.240/.327/.355
2017	SLN	MLB	26	411	55	27	3	4	42	41	60	8	2	.285/.376/.412
2018	SLN	MLB	27	407	41	18	2	9	38	31	60	6	5	.249/.332/.388
2019	SLN	MLB	28	418	47	17	2	8	39	37	66	8	3	.249/.333/.372

Breakout: 2% Improve: 51% Collapse: 9% Attrition: 3% MLB: 98%
Comparables: Aaron Hill, Brian Roberts, Roberto Alomar

Wong's efforts to make more use of his compact build and natural bat speed have gone more or less for naught. He continues to morph into an extreme ground-ball hitter, and as a left-handed batter, that makes him very vulnerable to the shift. He laid down 20 bunts in 2018 but didn't turn them into enough hits to change either his stat line or opponents' strategies. Thus, he's becoming increasingly patient (a pessimist might call it passive, or even timid) as he tries to work walks and wait for a pitch he can hammer. He remains an unorthodox but highly effective defender at second base, however. A grinder at the plate who can comfortably rove for grounders, line drives and pop-ups in the field has real value, though with a low ceiling.

YEAR	TEAM	LVL	AGE	PA	DRC+	VORP	BABIP	BRR	FRAA	WARP
2016	MEM	AAA	25	34	215	11.0	.444	0.7	2B(4): 0.1, CF(3): 0.2	0.6
2016	SLN	MLB	25	361	90	14.5	.268	1.4	2B(88): 12.6, CF(8): -0.5	2.0
2017	SLN	MLB	26	411	97	23.3	.331	1.6	2B(106): -4.6	0.8
2018	SLN	MLB	27	407	91	11.5	.275	-2.0	2B(119): 6.0	1.2
2019	SLN	MLB	28	418	99	14.6	.282	0.0	2B 5	1.9

Kolten Wong, continued

Batted Ball Distribution

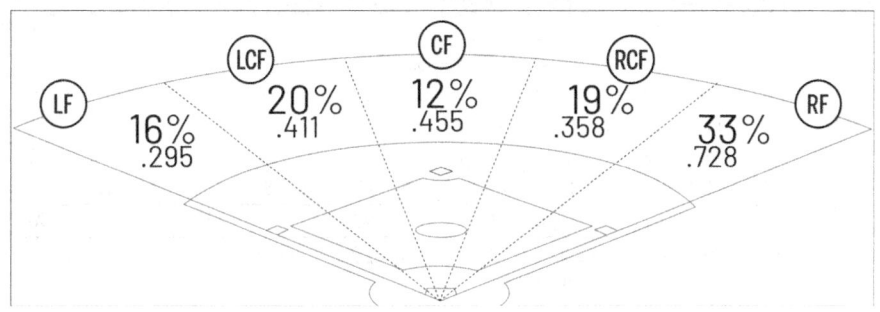

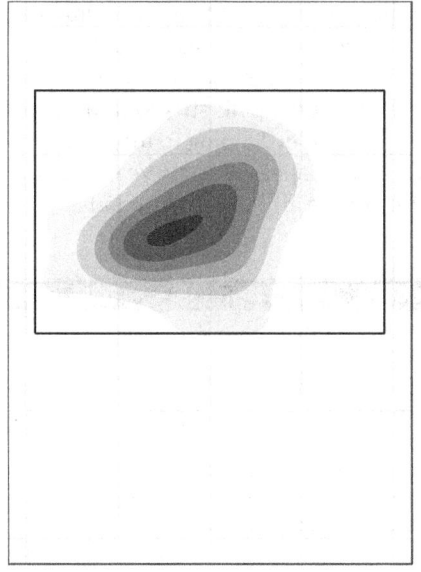

Strike Zone vs LHP

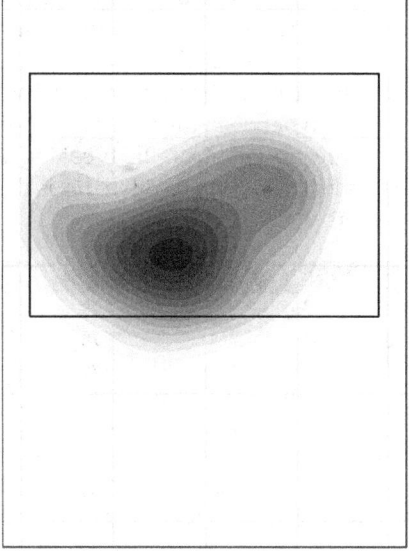

Strike Zone vs RHP

St. Louis Cardinals 2019

John Brebbia RHP

Born: 05/30/90   Age: 29   Bats: L   Throws: R
Height: 6'1"   Weight: 185   Origin: Round 30, 2011 Draft (#929 overall)

YEAR	TEAM	LVL	AGE	W	L	SV	G	GS	IP	H	HR	BB/9	K/9	K	GB%	BABIP
2016	SFD	AA	26	3	2	2	24	0	37.2	41	6	1.4	9.1	38	43%	.324
2016	MEM	AAA	26	2	3	0	19	0	30.1	41	3	3.9	8.9	30	46%	.396
2017	MEM	AAA	27	1	1	3	15	1	26.2	16	2	1.7	9.8	29	33%	.219
2017	SLN	MLB	27	0	0	0	50	0	51.2	37	8	1.9	8.9	51	26%	.216
2018	MEM	AAA	28	2	0	2	11	0	13.2	16	3	2.6	15.8	24	6%	.433
2018	SLN	MLB	28	3	3	2	45	0	50.2	43	5	2.8	10.7	60	33%	.297
2019	SLN	MLB	29	2	2	0	48	0	50	48	8	3.4	9.7	55	36%	.296

Breakout: 25%   Improve: 50%   Collapse: 13%   Attrition: 20%   MLB: 81%
Comparables: Jason Motte, Heath Bell, Matt Reynolds

During the winter of 2017-18, Brebbia shaved the beard for which he had become famous (he wasn't quite good enough to be famous for anything else) during his rookie season. Arguably more importantly, though, he also spent that time reshaping his slider and redesigning the interaction of that pitch with his four-seam heater. Leaning almost entirely on those two pitches (though undeniably aided by the impressive regrowth of the beard, in more or less the same shape it had been in before), Brebbia ratcheted up his strikeout rate. The separation between the fastball and slider grew wider, leading to more whiffs and more grounders on the breaking pitch. His facial hair is a few years late to the party, but Brebbia's pitch mix is the state of the art for right-handed relievers.

YEAR	TEAM	LVL	AGE	WHIP	ERA	DRA	WARP	MPH	FB%	WHF	CSP
2016	SFD	AA	26	1.25	4.06	3.55	0.5				
2016	MEM	AAA	26	1.78	6.23	2.80	0.8				
2017	MEM	AAA	27	0.79	1.69	3.10	0.7				
2017	SLN	MLB	27	0.93	2.44	4.60	0.3	96.0	56.7	13.5	49.2
2018	MEM	AAA	28	1.46	4.61	1.38	0.6				
2018	SLN	MLB	28	1.16	3.20	2.92	1.2	96.7	53.3	13.8	49.8
2019	SLN	MLB	29	1.32	4.40	4.70	0.1	95.7	54.7	13.7	49.5

John Brebbia, continued

Pitch Shape vs LHH

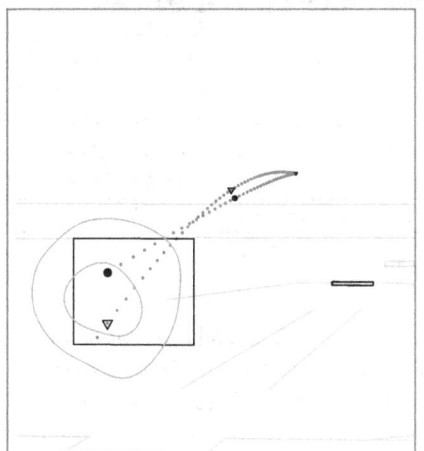

Pitch Shape vs RHH

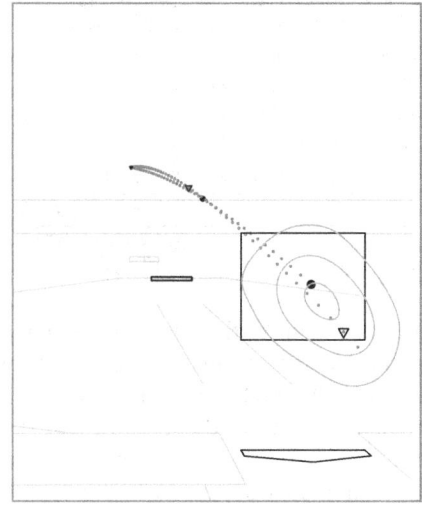

Type	Frequency	Velocity	H Movement	V Movement
● Fastball	51.7%	95.2 [109]	-8 [94]	-11.6 [113]
☐ Sinker	1.6%	93.9 [107]	-13.9 [89]	-18.9 [105]
+ Cutter				
▲ Changeup	1.3%	89 [115]	-12.4 [94]	-22.5 [114]
✕ Splitter				
▽ Slider	45.4%	83.3 [95]	8 [113]	-34 [97]
◇ Curveball				
✦ Slow Curveball				
✱ Knuckleball				
▼ Screwball				

St. Louis Cardinals 2019

Jack Flaherty   RHP
Born: 10/15/95   Age: 23   Bats: R   Throws: R
Height: 6'4"   Weight: 205   Origin: Round 1, 2014 Draft (#34 overall)

YEAR	TEAM	LVL	AGE	W	L	SV	G	GS	IP	H	HR	BB/9	K/9	K	GB%	BABIP
2016	PMB	A+	20	5	9	0	24	23	134	129	8	3.0	8.5	126	49%	.316
2017	SFD	AA	21	7	2	0	10	10	63^1	47	2	1.6	8.8	62	41%	.269
2017	MEM	AAA	21	7	2	0	15	15	85^1	73	10	2.5	9.0	85	42%	.288
2017	SLN	MLB	21	0	2	0	6	5	21^1	23	4	4.2	8.4	20	49%	.322
2018	MEM	AAA	22	4	1	0	5	5	31^2	22	2	2.0	11.7	41	44%	.274
2018	SLN	MLB	22	8	9	0	28	28	151	108	20	3.5	10.8	182	43%	.257
2019	SLN	MLB	23	12	8	0	28	28	168	136	16	3.2	10.2	190	43%	.288

Breakout: 22%   Improve: 58%   Collapse: 15%   Attrition: 14%   MLB: 85%
Comparables: Shelby Miller, Rubby De La Rosa, Luis Severino

We're all living in the Age of the Slider. Major League Baseball is a four-seam fastball-slider league. Some pitchers can succeed without one, but it's hard. Pitchers who do have one but can't rely on it (because it doesn't play well enough off their fastball, or because they can't throw it for a strike, or because they lack the feel to change its shape or throw it consistently without hanging too many) are doomed to the back ends of rotations or the low-leverage departments of bullpens. Flaherty is no longer classed with those guys. He's capable of throwing both his curve and his slider for a strike, putting hitters on the defensive. He's repeating the release point and consistently landing the slider where he wants it. It's a badass bat-misser, and his ticket to the top tier of NL starters.

YEAR	TEAM	LVL	AGE	WHIP	ERA	DRA	WARP	MPH	FB%	WHF	CSP
2016	PMB	A+	20	1.30	3.56	3.64	2.8				
2017	SFD	AA	21	0.92	1.42	3.28	1.4				
2017	MEM	AAA	21	1.14	2.74	3.42	2.1				
2017	SLN	MLB	21	1.55	6.33	3.28	0.5	94.9	55.9	14	47.2
2018	MEM	AAA	22	0.92	2.27	1.70	1.4				
2018	SLN	MLB	22	1.11	3.34	3.07	3.9	95.6	55.3	14.5	46
2019	SLN	MLB	23	1.15	3.30	3.66	2.7	95.4	57.3	15	48.2

Jack Flaherty, continued

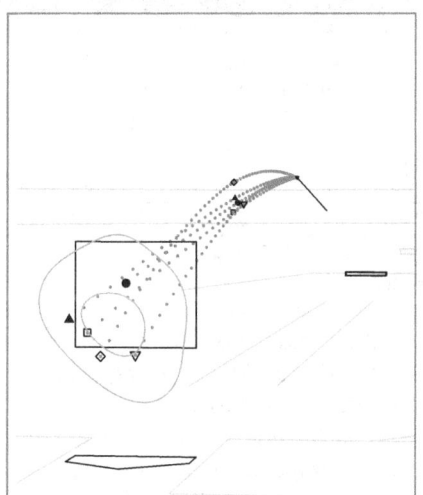
Pitch Shape vs LHH

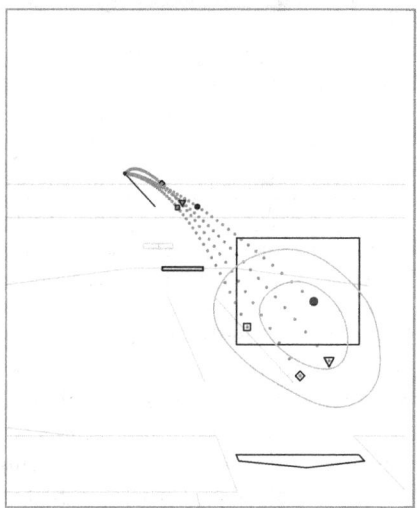
Pitch Shape vs RHH

Type	Frequency	Velocity	H Movement	V Movement
● Fastball	39.9%	93.8 [104]	-3.9 [113]	-14.8 [103]
☐ Sinker	15.3%	91.8 [97]	-10.6 [116]	-21.6 [96]
+ Cutter				
▲ Changeup	3.7%	86.5 [105]	-10.6 [104]	-26.3 [103]
✕ Splitter				
▽ Slider	29.9%	84.1 [99]	5.3 [102]	-30.8 [107]
◇ Curveball	11.2%	77.7 [97]	12.4 [119]	-51.1 [93]
⊕ Slow Curveball				
✳ Knuckleball				
▼ Screwball				

St. Louis Cardinals 2019

John Gant RHP

Born: 08/06/92   Age: 26   Bats: R   Throws: R
Height: 6'3"   Weight: 200   Origin: Round 21, 2011 Draft (#642 overall)

YEAR	TEAM	LVL	AGE	W	L	SV	G	GS	IP	H	HR	BB/9	K/9	K	GB%	BABIP
2016	GWN	AAA	23	3	3	0	12	10	56	58	5	3.5	9.2	57	49%	.329
2016	ATL	MLB	23	1	4	0	20	7	50	54	7	3.8	8.8	49	45%	.329
2017	MEM	AAA	24	6	5	0	18	18	103[1]	109	10	2.2	8.6	99	47%	.334
2017	SLN	MLB	24	0	1	0	7	2	17[1]	17	4	5.2	5.7	11	54%	.260
2018	MEM	AAA	25	5	1	0	8	8	49	45	5	2.9	7.7	42	49%	.288
2018	SLN	MLB	25	7	6	0	26	19	114	91	9	4.5	7.5	95	46%	.253
2019	SLN	MLB	26	5	5	0	38	11	86	84	10	3.8	8.1	78	46%	.295

Breakout: 25%   Improve: 51%   Collapse: 17%   Attrition: 22%   MLB: 83%
Comparables: Trevor Williams, Brock Stewart, James Paxton

Gant provides plenty to like. He employed a three-pitch mix (four-seamer, changeup, curve) until early in 2018, when he added a slider to the equation. All four pitches can miss bats, though none are true out pitches, and the spin rate on that fastball is one of the game's highest. He's tall and sturdily built, and he uses that frame well. Everything has life; batters don't square him up often. So far, his control hasn't withstood the test of big-league hitters' plate discipline all that well, but he's going to get several more shots to reach his ceiling in the middle of a rotation. There's a fair chance he even reaches it, at least for a little while.

YEAR	TEAM	LVL	AGE	WHIP	ERA	DRA	WARP	MPH	FB%	WHF	CSP
2016	GWN	AAA	23	1.43	4.18	3.25	1.3				
2016	ATL	MLB	23	1.50	4.86	4.04	0.7	94.4	58.5	10.7	47.5
2017	MEM	AAA	24	1.30	3.83	2.57	3.6				
2017	SLN	MLB	24	1.56	4.67	5.03	0.1	95.5	65.2	11	46.1
2018	MEM	AAA	25	1.24	1.65	3.08	1.4				
2018	SLN	MLB	25	1.30	3.47	4.05	1.6	95.4	55.4	12.2	48.5
2019	SLN	MLB	26	1.39	4.31	4.70	0.3	94.8	57.9	12	48.3

John Gant, continued

Pitch Shape vs LHH

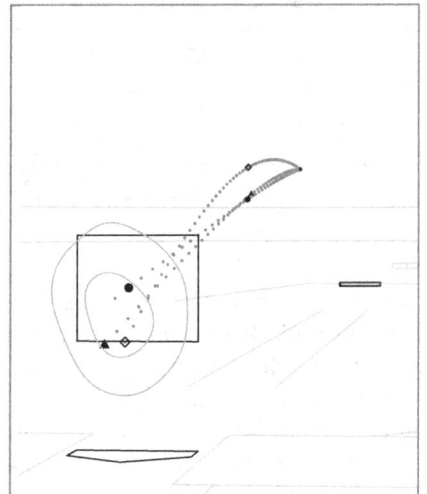

Pitch Shape vs RHH

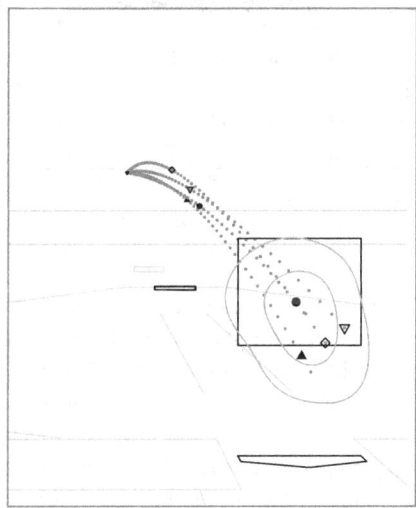

Type	Frequency	Velocity	H Movement	V Movement
● Fastball	55.4%	93.8 [104]	-12 [75]	-15.3 [101]
☐ Sinker				
+ Cutter				
▲ Changeup	27.5%	82 [87]	-10.1 [106]	-30.6 [90]
✕ Splitter				
▽ Slider	5.1%	83.9 [97]	3.2 [93]	-34.5 [96]
◇ Curveball	12.0%	76.6 [93]	8 [101]	-54.4 [86]
⊕ Slow Curveball				
✳ Knuckleball				
▼ Screwball				

Austin Gomber LHP

Born: 11/23/93 Age: 25 Bats: L Throws: L
Height: 6'5" Weight: 230 Origin: Round 4, 2014 Draft (#135 overall)

YEAR	TEAM	LVL	AGE	W	L	SV	G	GS	IP	H	HR	BB/9	K/9	K	GB%	BABIP
2016	PMB	A+	22	6	8	0	17	17	107^2	91	5	2.0	8.4	101	42%	.287
2016	SFD	AA	22	1	0	0	4	4	19^1	11	0	4.2	7.0	15	38%	.212
2017	SFD	AA	23	10	7	0	26	26	143	116	17	3.2	8.8	140	42%	.263
2018	MEM	AAA	24	7	3	0	12	11	68^1	65	9	2.6	10.0	76	40%	.311
2018	SLN	MLB	24	6	2	0	29	11	75	81	7	3.8	8.0	67	41%	.330
2019	SLN	MLB	25	4	4	0	21	10	61^1	59	9	3.4	8.4	57	40%	.291

Breakout: 11% Improve: 40% Collapse: 24% Attrition: 36% MLB: 79%
Comparables: Rafael Montero, Brandon Woodruff, Wade LeBlanc

The only truly above-average skill on the scouting report for Gomber is his command, though often, that turns out to be the most effective weapon even for pitchers with much better stuff. In Gomber's case, there are things the good command can't fix, like a changeup with virtually zero movement off a too-straight fastball, making both pitches reliant on fooling batters with the velocity separation between them. There are other things with which it does really help, though. Gomber moved to the first-base side of the rubber during a July demotion to Triple-A, changing the angle on that fastball-changeup sequence for righties and sharpening the difficulty of picking up his slider for lefties. Still, he has to execute perfectly, and even when he does, he doesn't really dominate.

YEAR	TEAM	LVL	AGE	WHIP	ERA	DRA	WARP	MPH	FB%	WHF	CSP
2016	PMB	A+	22	1.07	2.93	3.04	3.0				
2016	SFD	AA	22	1.03	1.40	4.09	0.2				
2017	SFD	AA	23	1.17	3.34	3.36	3.1				
2018	MEM	AAA	24	1.24	3.42	2.74	2.1				
2018	SLN	MLB	24	1.51	4.44	4.95	0.2	94.8	50.4	10	49.8
2019	SLN	MLB	25	1.32	4.45	4.86	0.1	94.5	51.6	10.2	51

Austin Gomber, continued

Pitch Shape vs LHH

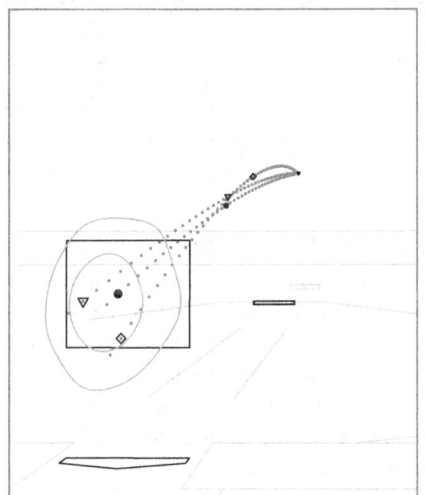

Pitch Shape vs RHH

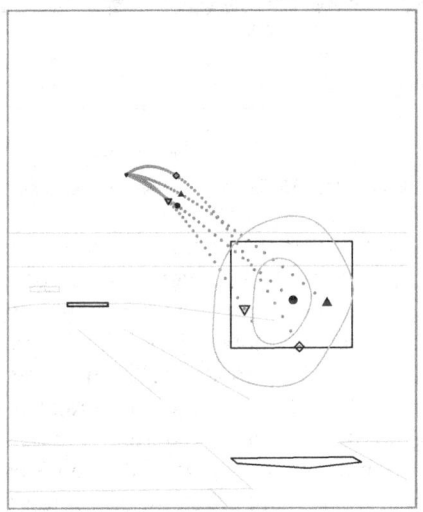

Type	Frequency	Velocity	H Movement	V Movement
● Fastball	50.4%	92.9 [101]	7.4 [97]	-13.4 [108]
☐ Sinker				
+ Cutter	0.9%	90.5 [110]	-0.9 [94]	-19.3 [118]
▲ Changeup	8.0%	83.9 [94]	7.1 [122]	-21.7 [117]
✕ Splitter				
▽ Slider	19.0%	89 [120]	-2.4 [89]	-22.2 [132]
◇ Curveball	21.7%	78.2 [99]	-4.6 [87]	-51 [93]
⊕ Slow Curveball				
✳ Knuckleball				
▼ Screwball				

Luke Gregerson RHP

Born: 05/14/84 Age: 35 Bats: L Throws: R
Height: 6'3" Weight: 205 Origin: Round 28, 2006 Draft (#856 overall)

YEAR	TEAM	LVL	AGE	W	L	SV	G	GS	IP	H	HR	BB/9	K/9	K	GB%	BABIP
2016	HOU	MLB	32	4	3	15	59	0	57²	38	5	2.8	10.5	67	62%	.239
2017	HOU	MLB	33	2	3	1	65	0	61	62	13	3.0	10.3	70	49%	.306
2018	SLN	MLB	34	0	0	0	17	0	12²	14	2	4.3	8.5	12	56%	.324
2019	SLN	MLB	35	2	2	0	37	0	39	36	5	4.0	8.6	38	51%	.291

Breakout: 25% Improve: 48% Collapse: 24% Attrition: 10% MLB: 92%
Comparables: Kyle Farnsworth, Gary Lavelle, Rollie Fingers

One of the originators of the slider revolution that has created the new world order of baseball, Gregerson is still dependent upon that pitch for success. As he wades deeper into his mid-30s, though, it's harder and harder for him to hold onto his trademark. Injuries finally truly truncated a season for him, for the first time in his 10 campaigns. When he was on the mound, his sinker was down to about 88 miles per hour, on average. It's a heavy pitch that induces tons of grounders, but it gives batters time to wait and suss out what's coming. The widening movement gap between Gregerson's sinker and slider only exacerbates that problem. Unless full health restores some zip to the heat or bite to the slider, he's permanently (if marginally) diminished.

YEAR	TEAM	LVL	AGE	WHIP	ERA	DRA	WARP	MPH	FB%	WHF	CSP
2016	HOU	MLB	32	0.97	3.28	2.36	1.7	91.4	53.4	20.6	41.5
2017	HOU	MLB	33	1.34	4.57	4.08	0.7	90.8	52.3	17.1	43.1
2018	SLN	MLB	34	1.58	7.11	3.25	0.2	89.0	64.7	13	40.5
2019	SLN	MLB	35	1.36	4.27	4.60	0.1	89.6	53.5	17.4	40.9

Luke Gregerson, continued

Pitch Shape vs LHH	Pitch Shape vs RHH
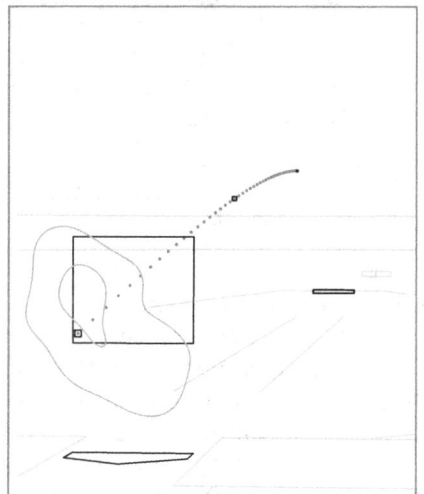	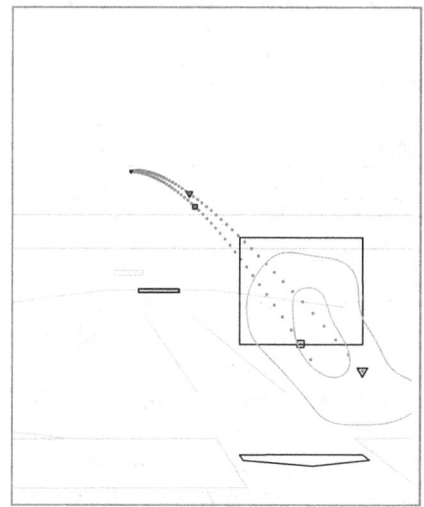

Type	Frequency	Velocity	H Movement	V Movement
● Fastball	19.8%	88.2 [86]	-0.9 [127]	-22.3 [79]
☐ Sinker	44.9%	88.4 [80]	-8.2 [137]	-26.4 [80]
+ Cutter				
▲ Changeup	1.0%	79.3 [76]	-10.4 [104]	-36.4 [73]
✕ Splitter				
▽ Slider	34.3%	81 [85]	7.6 [112]	-38 [85]
◇ Curveball				
⊕ Slow Curveball				
✳ Knuckleball				
▼ Screwball				

St. Louis Cardinals 2019

Jordan Hicks   RHP
Born: 09/06/96   Age: 22   Bats: R   Throws: R
Height: 6'2"   Weight: 185   Origin: Round SUP, 2015 Draft (#105 overall)

YEAR	TEAM	LVL	AGE	W	L	SV	G	GS	IP	H	HR	BB/9	K/9	K	GB%	BABIP
2016	JCY	RK	19	2	1	0	6	6	30	33	1	3.9	6.0	20	57%	.344
2016	SCO	A-	19	4	1	0	6	6	30^2	25	0	4.7	6.5	22	66%	.269
2017	PEO	A	20	8	2	0	14	14	78	75	3	4.5	7.3	63	53%	.316
2017	PMB	A+	20	0	1	1	8	5	27	21	0	2.0	10.7	32	67%	.318
2018	SLN	MLB	21	3	4	6	73	0	77^2	59	2	5.2	8.1	70	62%	.266
2019	SLN	MLB	22	3	3	14	53	0	56^1	50	5	5.4	8.3	52	53%	.292

Breakout: 20%   Improve: 28%   Collapse: 12%   Attrition: 19%   MLB: 60%
Comparables: Jenrry Mejia, Lance McCullers, Mike Montgomery

Hicks didn't pitch at all in the upper minors before getting promoted into the St. Louis bullpen for Opening Day of 2018. It should come as no surprise, then, that he's still an unfinished product. His rookie campaign was attention-grabbing, as he demonstrated the ability to consistently throw harder than anyone this side of Peak Aroldis Chapman. What he didn't demonstrate the ability to do, however, might be more important. Hicks didn't miss bats with any consistency, and he didn't throw enough strikes to get away with that, especially as his first season as a reliever wore him down. His slider induced whiffs on over half of opponents' swings, but he threw his sinker nearly three times as often as that slider. Heavy reliance on a fastball, especially a sinker, just doesn't permit one to succeed in MLB anymore, no matter how hard it's thrown. There's more to the fastball than being fast.

YEAR	TEAM	LVL	AGE	WHIP	ERA	DRA	WARP	MPH	FB%	WHF	CSP
2016	JCY	RK	19	1.53	4.20	5.03	0.2				
2016	SCO	A-	19	1.34	1.76	3.92	0.5				
2017	PEO	A	20	1.46	3.35	6.50	-1.1				
2017	PMB	A+	20	1.00	1.00	2.19	1.0				
2018	SLN	MLB	21	1.34	3.59	6.03	-1.0	102.9	78	10.1	47.1
2019	SLN	MLB	22	1.48	4.52	4.81	0.0	102.9	81.3	10.6	49.1

Jordan Hicks, continued

Pitch Shape vs LHH

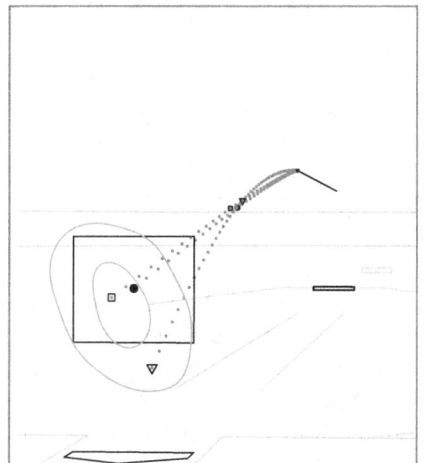

Pitch Shape vs RHH

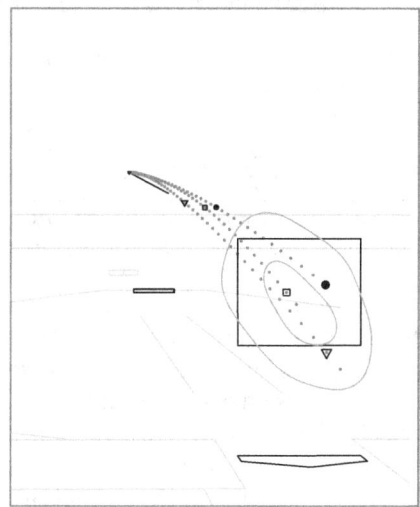

Type	Frequency	Velocity	H Movement	V Movement
● Fastball	6.0%	101.7 [130]	-8 [94]	-12.5 [110]
□ Sinker	72.1%	101 [143]	-12.2 [103]	-16.7 [112]
+ Cutter				
▲ Changeup				
✕ Splitter				
▽ Slider	21.8%	86.8 [110]	10.6 [125]	-33.7 [98]
◇ Curveball	0.2%	83.6 [119]	7.7 [99]	-44.3 [108]
✢ Slow Curveball				
✱ Knuckleball				
▼ Screwball				

Dakota Hudson RHP

Born: 09/15/94 Age: 24 Bats: R Throws: R
Height: 6'5" Weight: 215 Origin: Round 1, 2016 Draft (#34 overall)

YEAR	TEAM	LVL	AGE	W	L	SV	G	GS	IP	H	HR	BB/9	K/9	K	GB%	BABIP
2016	PMB	A+	21	1	1	3	8	0	9^1	6	0	6.8	9.6	10	91%	.261
2017	SFD	AA	22	9	4	0	18	18	114	111	5	2.7	6.1	77	58%	.296
2017	MEM	AAA	22	1	1	0	7	7	38^2	36	2	3.5	4.4	19	59%	.272
2018	MEM	AAA	23	13	3	0	19	19	111^2	107	1	3.1	7.0	87	59%	.313
2018	SLN	MLB	23	4	1	0	26	0	27^1	19	0	5.9	6.3	19	64%	.237
2019	SLN	MLB	24	3	3	0	53	0	56^1	48	4	4.3	8.1	51	56%	.283

Breakout: 16% Improve: 35% Collapse: 27% Attrition: 44% MLB: 75%
Comparables: Jarred Cosart, Paul Blackburn, Chi Chi Gonzalez

One of baseball's most delightful mysteries is that some pitchers are more than the sum of their parts—a better full package than the individual items on their scouting checklist suggest. Alas, the Newtonian universe requires that there be some pitchers on the other side of the equation, even if they have the mental and physical tools and can more or less find the strike zone. That's Hudson. His four-seam fastball is a little too straight to miss bats, despite its good velocity. His sinker has good run, but he doesn't command it well, at least at this stage. His cutter is hard and generates plenty of grounders, but doesn't generate enough whiffs, either. Unless Hudson can reshape something in his repertoire or tighten his command, he's doomed to tantalizing but non-dominant relief work.

YEAR	TEAM	LVL	AGE	WHIP	ERA	DRA	WARP	MPH	FB%	WHF	CSP
2016	PMB	A+	21	1.39	0.96	3.07	0.2				
2017	SFD	AA	22	1.27	2.53	5.76	-0.8				
2017	MEM	AAA	22	1.32	4.42	5.27	0.2				
2018	MEM	AAA	23	1.30	2.50	3.50	2.6				
2018	SLN	MLB	23	1.35	2.63	6.41	-0.5	97.3	60.7	9.9	47.3
2019	SLN	MLB	24	1.32	3.97	4.36	0.3	97.1	62.6	10.2	48.7

Dakota Hudson, continued

Pitch Shape vs LHH	Pitch Shape vs RHH
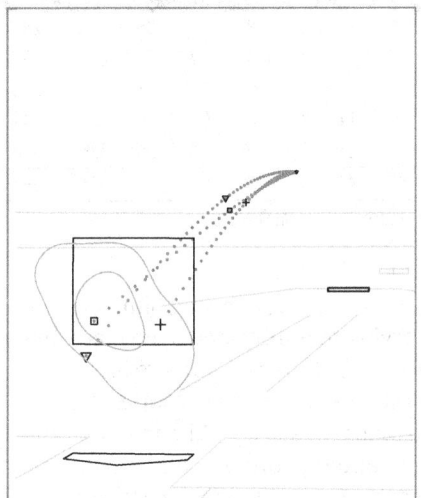	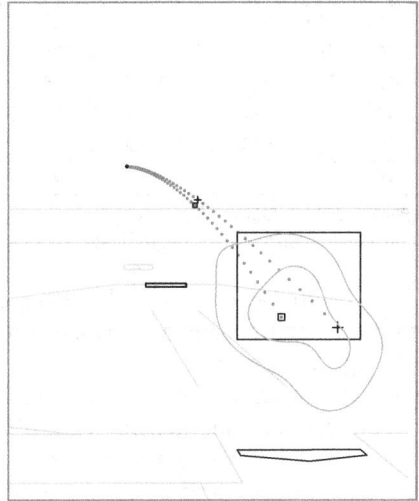

Type	Frequency	Velocity	H Movement	V Movement
● Fastball	2.3%	97.5 [116]	-3.3 [116]	-13.3 [108]
☐ Sinker	58.4%	96.4 [120]	-11.4 [110]	-19.8 [102]
+ Cutter	28.6%	91.6 [117]	2.9 [106]	-25.5 [93]
▲ Changeup				
✕ Splitter				
▽ Slider	10.6%	87 [111]	6.2 [106]	-33.4 [99]
◇ Curveball				
⊕ Slow Curveball				
✱ Knuckleball				
▼ Screwball				

St. Louis Cardinals 2019

Dominic Leone RHP

Born: 10/26/91 Age: 27 Bats: R Throws: R
Height: 5'11" Weight: 210 Origin: Round 16, 2012 Draft (#491 overall)

YEAR	TEAM	LVL	AGE	W	L	SV	G	GS	IP	H	HR	BB/9	K/9	K	GB%	BABIP
2016	RNO	AAA	24	5	2	1	33	0	35	25	4	2.8	9.3	36	36%	.247
2016	ARI	MLB	24	0	1	0	25	0	27	45	7	4.0	7.7	23	47%	.432
2017	TOR	MLB	25	3	0	1	65	0	70.1	51	6	2.9	10.4	81	41%	.266
2018	MEM	AAA	26	1	1	0	10	0	10	14	3	5.4	6.3	7	37%	.344
2018	SLN	MLB	26	1	2	0	29	0	24	27	3	3.0	9.8	26	32%	.348
2019	SLN	MLB	27	2	2	0	43	0	45	44	6	4.2	8.9	44	39%	.297

Breakout: 34%   Improve: 57%   Collapse: 20%   Attrition: 28%   MLB: 91%
Comparables: Boone Logan, Sergio Santos, Ian Krol

Leone's cutter emerged as a dominant offering in 2017, allowing him to attack left-handed hitters and miss a lot of bats. Trying to double down, he made that offering more prominent in his arsenal in 2018, but the results were less impressive. As many pitchers have under the tutelage of Mike Maddux, Leone saw his fastball straighten out a bit, which made it easier for him to pound the strike zone but lowered a whiff rate that was already suboptimal, even for a fastball. His sinker didn't induce grounders the way it had in the past, and he became an extreme fly-ball guy. Worse, he failed to demonstrate the durability required of back-end relievers. Leone needs another tweak to that cutter (perhaps a move back toward the slider he used to throw) in order to be more than a marginal middle reliever again.

YEAR	TEAM	LVL	AGE	WHIP	ERA	DRA	WARP	MPH	FB%	WHF	CSP
2016	RNO	AAA	24	1.03	3.34	3.65	0.5				
2016	ARI	MLB	24	2.11	6.33	5.48	-0.2	95.2	82.7	12.9	47.9
2017	TOR	MLB	25	1.05	2.56	3.07	1.6	95.9	90.4	16	44
2018	MEM	AAA	26	2.00	7.20	3.06	0.2				
2018	SLN	MLB	26	1.46	4.50	4.03	0.2	95.7	95.4	15.7	45.9
2019	SLN	MLB	27	1.44	4.82	5.03	-0.1	95.3	91.3	15.5	46.3

Dominic Leone, continued

Pitch Shape vs LHH

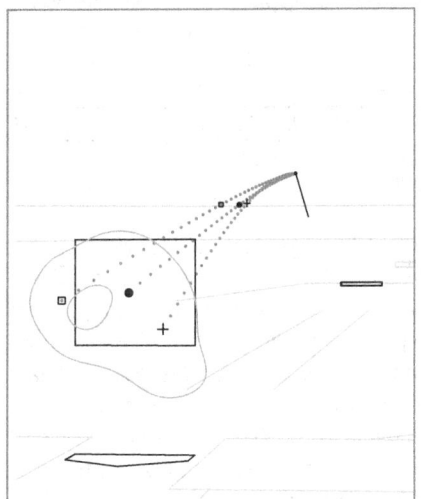

Pitch Shape vs RHH

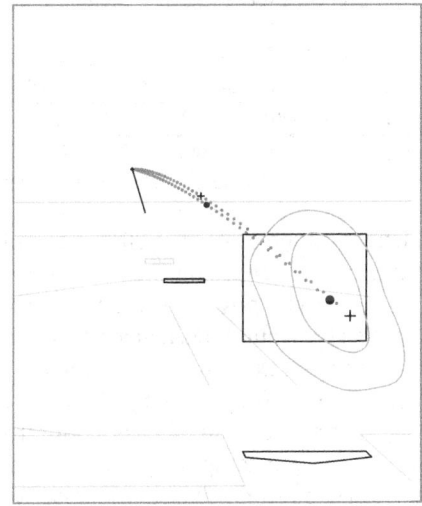

Type	Frequency	Velocity	H Movement	V Movement
● Fastball	31.1%	94.6 [107]	-4.3 [111]	-12.8 [109]
☐ Sinker	26.0%	94.3 [109]	-11.7 [107]	-16.6 [112]
+ Cutter	38.3%	89.4 [104]	4.4 [115]	-25.1 [94]
▲ Changeup				
✕ Splitter				
▽ Slider	4.6%	84.3 [99]	5.4 [102]	-36.4 [90]
◇ Curveball				
✥ Slow Curveball				
✱ Knuckleball				
▼ Screwball				

St. Louis Cardinals 2019

Carlos Martinez RHP

Born: 09/21/91 Age: 27 Bats: R Throws: R
Height: 6'0" Weight: 190 Origin: International Free Agent, 2009

YEAR	TEAM	LVL	AGE	W	L	SV	G	GS	IP	H	HR	BB/9	K/9	K	GB%	BABIP
2016	SLN	MLB	24	16	9	0	31	31	195^1	169	15	3.2	8.0	174	58%	.286
2017	SLN	MLB	25	12	11	0	32	32	205	179	27	3.1	9.5	217	52%	.285
2018	SLN	MLB	26	8	6	5	33	18	118^2	100	5	4.6	8.9	117	51%	.290
2019	SLN	MLB	27	9	7	0	24	24	127	111	12	3.5	9.0	127	51%	.291

Breakout: 14% Improve: 54% Collapse: 22% Attrition: 5% MLB: 97%
Comparables: Johnny Antonelli, Felix Hernandez, Alex Wood

Martinez added a cutter in 2018. Now, please, don't get too excited. New pitches in the arsenal are to Martinez as Horcruxes are to Voldemort: they technically make him more powerful and harder to kill, but they also cost something. They diminish him, numb his feel for each little piece of the larger repertoire. He's able to pound the zone, more often than not, but his command is less fine than ever. Worse, perhaps, the injuries that cost Martinez part of 2018 also seem to have sapped a couple miles per hour from his fastball. The mid-season move to the bullpen was temporary, but his velocity drop and tumble out of the top echelon of starters are both more likely to be permanent.

YEAR	TEAM	LVL	AGE	WHIP	ERA	DRA	WARP	MPH	FB%	WHF	CSP
2016	SLN	MLB	24	1.22	3.04	3.46	4.2	99.6	58.3	10.7	49.1
2017	SLN	MLB	25	1.22	3.64	3.43	4.9	98.8	56.3	11.6	50.8
2018	SLN	MLB	26	1.35	3.11	4.63	0.9	97.0	44.2	11.7	48.9
2019	SLN	MLB	27	1.26	3.66	4.05	1.5	98.0	53.7	11.5	50.2

Carlos Martinez, continued

Pitch Shape vs LHH	Pitch Shape vs RHH
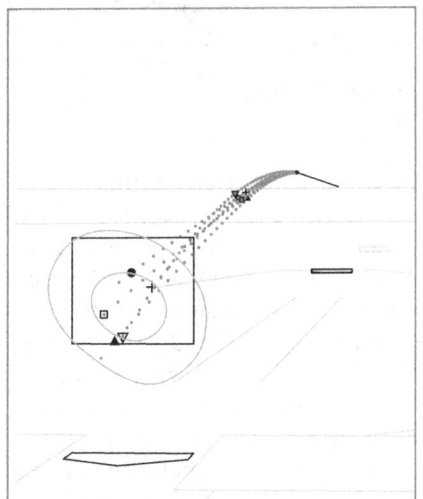	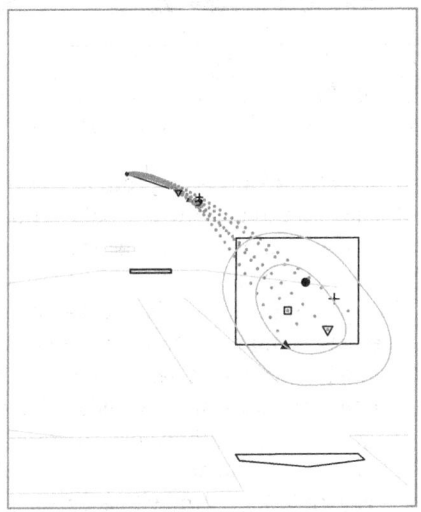

Type	Frequency	Velocity	H Movement	V Movement
● Fastball	17.8%	95.6 [110]	-5.1 [107]	-14.9 [103]
☐ Sinker	26.3%	93 [103]	-13.2 [95]	-23.9 [88]
+ Cutter	17.4%	91.3 [115]	0.6 [93]	-22.8 [104]
▲ Changeup	13.2%	87.2 [108]	-12.2 [95]	-33.5 [82]
✕ Splitter				
▽ Slider	23.6%	83.8 [97]	10.9 [126]	-32.8 [101]
◇ Curveball	1.6%	78.8 [101]	10.8 [112]	-40.2 [118]
⊕ Slow Curveball				
✳ Knuckleball				
▼ Screwball				

Miles Mikolas   RHP

Born: 08/23/88   Age: 30   Bats: R   Throws: R
Height: 6'5"   Weight: 220   Origin: Round 7, 2009 Draft (#204 overall)

YEAR	TEAM	LVL	AGE	W	L	SV	G	GS	IP	H	HR	BB/9	K/9	K	GB%	BABIP
2018	SLN	MLB	29	18	4	0	32	32	200^2	186	16	1.3	6.5	146	51%	.279
2019	SLN	MLB	30	11	9	0	28	28	168	161	18	2.0	7.2	134	49%	.288

Breakout: 18%   Improve: 53%   Collapse: 18%   Attrition: 8%   MLB: 94%
Comparables: Doug Fister, Brandon McCarthy, Hyun-jin Ryu

We rarely frame it this way, but in terms of pitch selection, MLB has moved a good distance in the direction of Nippon Professional Baseball over the last few years. When Mikolas returned from Japan in 2018, he was wired for success in the Majors in a way he and others who walked his path never had been before. He's comfortable using his four-seam fastball, his sinker, his slider, and his curveball—so much so that he threw all of them between 20 and 28 percent of the time last year. This has been the paradigm in the highest level of Japanese baseball for years, but MLB has tended to be a fastball-forward league. As it's changed of late, it's done so in the direction of favoring whichever dominant pitch a hurler has in his repertoire. Mikolas, lacking one overwhelming offering, blends excellent control with exceptional unpredictability, and keeps the ball on the ground. (It doesn't hurt that he's also throwing harder than ever.)

YEAR	TEAM	LVL	AGE	WHIP	ERA	DRA	WARP	MPH	FB%	WHF	CSP
2018	SLN	MLB	29	1.07	2.83	3.38	4.5	96.1	48.6	10.5	51.8
2019	SLN	MLB	30	1.16	3.69	4.10	1.9	95.3	48.5	10.5	51.7

Miles Mikolas, continued

Pitch Shape vs LHH

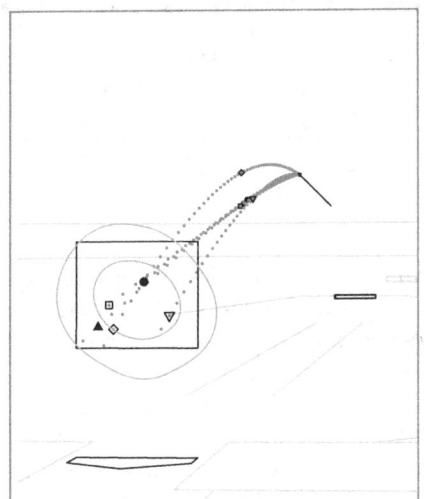

Pitch Shape vs RHH

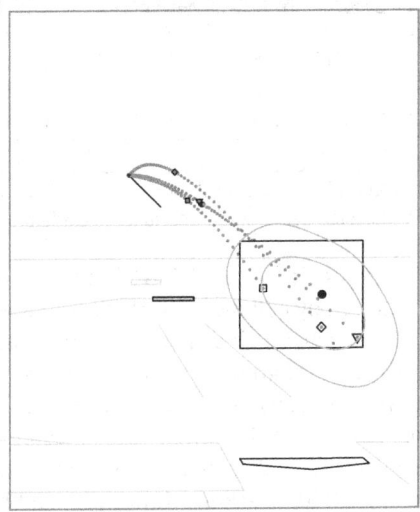

Type	Frequency	Velocity	H Movement	V Movement
● Fastball	26.6%	94.7 [107]	-3.9 [113]	-15 [102]
☐ Sinker	22.0%	94.1 [108]	-11.4 [110]	-17.7 [109]
+ Cutter				
▲ Changeup	4.2%	89 [115]	-12.6 [93]	-25.2 [106]
✕ Splitter				
▽ Slider	25.8%	88.5 [118]	3.4 [94]	-27.8 [115]
◇ Curveball	21.4%	78.9 [102]	8.5 [103]	-52.7 [90]
⊕ Slow Curveball				
✳ Knuckleball				
▼ Screwball				

Andrew Miller   LHP

Born: 05/21/85 Age: 34 Bats: L Throws: L
Height: 6'7" Weight: 205 Origin: Round 1, 2006 Draft (#6 overall)

YEAR	TEAM	LVL	AGE	W	L	SV	G	GS	IP	H	HR	BB/9	K/9	K	GB%	BABIP
2016	NYA	MLB	31	6	1	9	44	0	45^1	28	5	1.4	15.3	77	55%	.284
2016	CLE	MLB	31	4	0	3	26	0	29	14	3	0.6	14.3	46	58%	.212
2017	CLE	MLB	32	4	3	2	57	0	62^2	31	3	3.0	13.6	95	42%	.233
2018	CLE	MLB	33	2	4	2	37	0	34	31	3	4.2	11.9	45	50%	.329
2019	SLN	MLB	34	3	2	22	53	0	56^1	45	5	3.3	10.6	66	47%	.285

Breakout: 11% Improve: 27% Collapse: 43% Attrition: 7% MLB: 90%
Comparables: Seung Hwan Oh, Francisco Cordero, Jerry Blevins

Rembrandt's "Danae." The Library at Alexandria. Andrew Miller. Historic beauty shattered by callous misfortune and the violence and ugliness of the world, the brilliance of which can never truly be recreated, an idea as much as a memory, a byword to magnificence lost dwarfing the magnificence that once was. Okay, so, it probably says more about Miller's 2013-2017 run — which looked something like Randy Johnson in an Iron Man suit when totaled together — that his 2018 felt like such a disaster. When you step back, it was a half season hampered by injury. It's hard to know how much of his Quite Good But Not Superlative was a result of pitching at less than 100 percent. Perhaps an offseason of rest will restore him to his world consuming powers or maybe there was real decline here. With stuff as magisterial as Miller's, which took as long to harness as it did, there's always fear that when it goes it will go suddenly. Then again, with stuff as magisterial as Miller's, there's a whole lot of declining he'd have to do before he'd be anything resembling ineffective.

YEAR	TEAM	LVL	AGE	WHIP	ERA	DRA	WARP	MPH	FB%	WHF	CSP
2016	NYA	MLB	31	0.77	1.39	1.79	1.7	98.2	39.4	17.7	46.4
2016	CLE	MLB	31	0.55	1.55	2.07	1.0	97.5	39.7	15.8	49.5
2017	CLE	MLB	32	0.83	1.44	2.30	2.0	96.9	41.9	17.1	45.7
2018	CLE	MLB	33	1.38	4.24	3.08	0.7	95.5	43.3	13.7	50.2
2019	SLN	MLB	34	1.15	2.98	3.52	0.8	95.7	40.9	15.9	47.3

Andrew Miller, continued

Pitch Shape vs LHH   **Pitch Shape vs RHH**

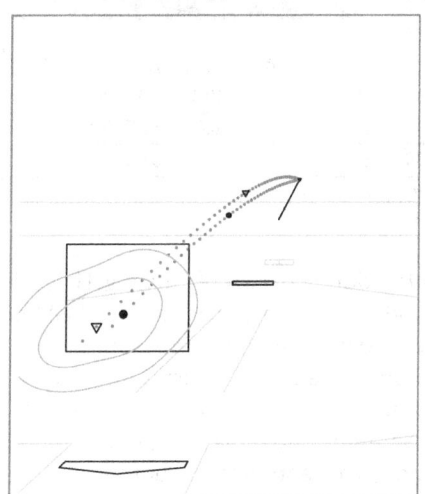 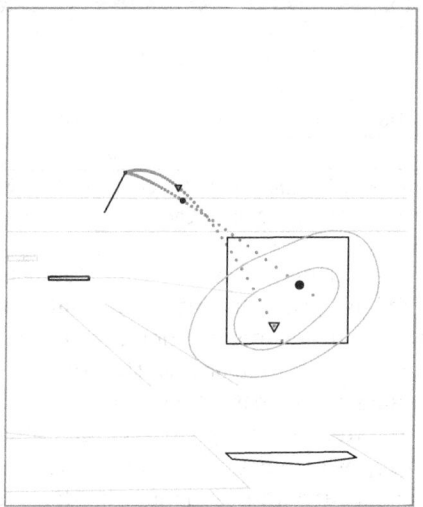

Type	Frequency	Velocity	H Movement	V Movement
● Fastball	43.3%	93.6 [103]	6.9 [99]	-14.8 [103]
☐ Sinker				
+ Cutter				
▲ Changeup				
✕ Splitter				
▽ Slider	56.7%	83.3 [95]	-9.3 [119]	-37 [88]
◇ Curveball				
⊕ Slow Curveball				
✳ Knuckleball				
▼ Screwball				

Daniel Poncedeleon RHP

Born: 01/16/92 Age: 27 Bats: R Throws: R
Height: 6'4" Weight: 185 Origin: Round 9, 2014 Draft (#285 overall)

YEAR	TEAM	LVL	AGE	W	L	SV	G	GS	IP	H	HR	BB/9	K/9	K	GB%	BABIP
2016	SFD	AA	24	9	8	0	27	27	151	128	10	3.3	7.3	122	46%	.269
2017	MEM	AAA	25	2	0	0	6	6	29	20	2	4.0	7.8	25	42%	.234
2018	MEM	AAA	26	9	4	0	19	18	96^1	69	4	4.7	10.3	110	30%	.272
2018	SLN	MLB	26	0	2	1	11	4	33	24	2	3.5	8.5	31	36%	.259
2019	SLN	MLB	27	3	3	0	37	5	58	51	8	4.1	9.3	61	38%	.284

Breakout: 3%   Improve: 17%   Collapse: 10%   Attrition: 18%   MLB: 36%
Comparables: Tyler Wagner, Chris Heston, Lucas Harrell

Poncedeleon makes for an interesting exploration of the art of pitching. He's tall and lanky, and can create some difficult angles for opposing batters. His fastball has good rise, though not much wiggle, so he'd be well-advised to work up with it more often than he has. There's a big curveball he doesn't trust, which is a shame, because it's the real eye-level changer of his pack of secondary pitches. His cutter and changeup have about the same sink and move the same amount, in opposite directions, off the heater, so there's deception there, but the cutter comes out of the hand much harder, and he doesn't disguise the arm action well. A couple adjustments could unlock a mid-rotation upside, but Poncedeleon should have made them by now. Unless he finds a fountain of youth, the stuff might soften too much before he can firm up his feel for it.

YEAR	TEAM	LVL	AGE	WHIP	ERA	DRA	WARP	MPH	FB%	WHF	CSP
2016	SFD	AA	24	1.22	3.52	4.03	1.9				
2017	MEM	AAA	25	1.14	2.17	5.21	0.2				
2018	MEM	AAA	26	1.24	2.24	3.89	1.8				
2018	SLN	MLB	26	1.12	2.73	3.52	0.6	95.4	61.8	14.5	49.8
2019	SLN	MLB	27	1.31	4.42	4.76	0.1	94.9	62.5	14.6	50.4

Daniel Poncedeleon, continued

Pitch Shape vs LHH

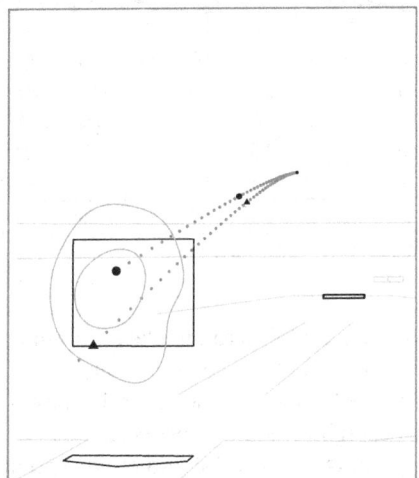

Pitch Shape vs RHH

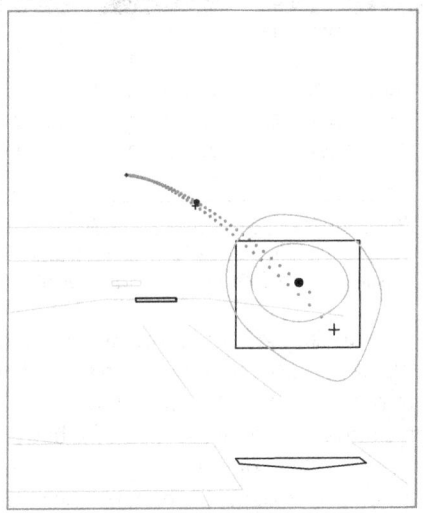

Type	Frequency	Velocity	H Movement	V Movement
● Fastball	61.8%	93.7 [104]	-9 [89]	-13.6 [107]
☐ Sinker				
+ Cutter	18.6%	90 [107]	-0.6 [85]	-22.7 [104]
▲ Changeup	16.5%	83.5 [93]	-14.2 [84]	-26.7 [102]
✕ Splitter				
▽ Slider				
◇ Curveball	3.1%	77.3 [96]	7.2 [97]	-56.5 [81]
✦ Slow Curveball				
✱ Knuckleball				
▼ Screwball				

St. Louis Cardinals 2019

Chasen Shreve LHP

Born: 07/12/90   Age: 28   Bats: L   Throws: L
Height: 6'4"   Weight: 195   Origin: Round 11, 2010 Draft (#344 overall)

YEAR	TEAM	LVL	AGE	W	L	SV	G	GS	IP	H	HR	BB/9	K/9	K	GB%	BABIP
2016	SWB	AAA	25	0	0	0	13	1	16²	4	1	3.8	10.8	20	46%	.094
2016	NYA	MLB	25	2	1	1	37	0	33	29	8	3.5	9.0	33	44%	.247
2017	SWB	AAA	26	1	0	1	9	0	11¹	7	0	2.4	15.1	19	48%	.333
2017	NYA	MLB	26	4	1	0	44	0	45¹	35	8	5.0	11.5	58	37%	.252
2018	NYA	MLB	27	2	2	1	40	0	38	39	8	4.3	10.9	46	49%	.320
2018	SLN	MLB	27	1	2	0	20	0	14²	14	3	5.5	9.8	16	22%	.297
2019	SLN	MLB	28	2	2	3	37	0	39	35	5	4.2	9.8	43	42%	.293

Breakout: 29%   Improve: 47%   Collapse: 24%   Attrition: 11%   MLB: 93%
Comparables: Tony Sipp, Ken Howell, Bill Caudill

If one doesn't get too mired in what Shreve isn't, there's a ton to like about him. He's never succeeded when stretched or challenged to take on too many innings, but he isn't confined to a matchup role, because his slider and splitter give him a secondary weapon for batters of each handedness (especially if his uptick in whiffs on the slider is for real). Repeating his arm slot and release point was once a struggle for him, but he really tightened that up in 2018. Shreve's going to give up too many home runs, and that's a fatal flaw for a high-leverage reliever, but he can deliver quality medium-leverage frames. His fastball looks pedestrian to a radar gun but preternatural to a TrackMan system, with a ton of spin. He'd thrive as a twice-weekly opener ahead of right-handed bulk guys.

YEAR	TEAM	LVL	AGE	WHIP	ERA	DRA	WARP	MPH	FB%	WHF	CSP
2016	SWB	AAA	25	0.66	1.62	1.85	0.6				
2016	NYA	MLB	25	1.27	5.18	3.68	0.5	93.8	50	14.7	37.1
2017	SWB	AAA	26	0.88	1.59	1.65	0.5				
2017	NYA	MLB	26	1.32	3.77	5.38	-0.1	94.3	49.2	15.4	36.5
2018	NYA	MLB	27	1.50	4.26	2.83	0.9	93.4	52.9	15.5	39.3
2018	SLN	MLB	27	1.57	3.07	5.39	-0.1	93.3	56.1	14.5	42.5
2019	SLN	MLB	28	1.35	4.05	4.43	0.2	93.2	51.9	15.3	38.4

Chasen Shreve, continued

Pitch Shape vs LHH   **Pitch Shape vs RHH**

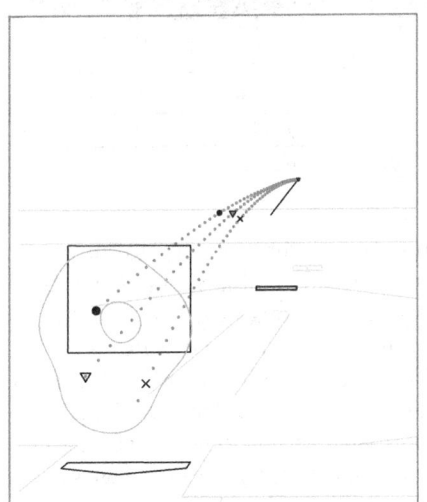 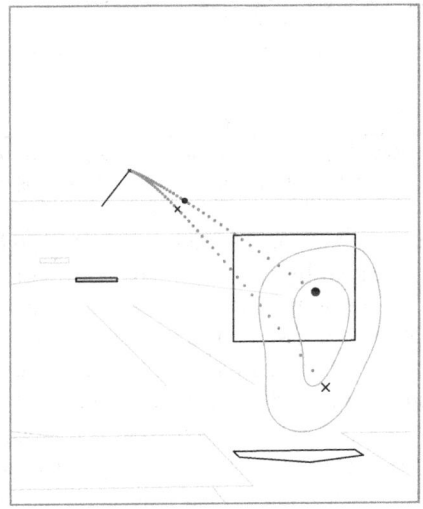

Type	Frequency	Velocity	H Movement	V Movement
● Fastball	53.7%	92.4 [100]	10.2 [84]	-13.3 [108]
□ Sinker				
+ Cutter				
▲ Changeup				
× Splitter	37.0%	84.7 [95]	11.7 [86]	-29.4 [101]
▽ Slider	9.3%	86.2 [108]	-0.2 [80]	-30.2 [108]
◇ Curveball				
⊕ Slow Curveball				
✳ Knuckleball				
▼ Screwball				

St. Louis Cardinals 2019

Michael Wacha   RHP
Born: 07/01/91   Age: 27   Bats: R   Throws: R
Height: 6'6"   Weight: 215   Origin: Round 1, 2012 Draft (#19 overall)

YEAR	TEAM	LVL	AGE	W	L	SV	G	GS	IP	H	HR	BB/9	K/9	K	GB%	BABIP
2016	SLN	MLB	24	7	7	0	27	24	138	159	15	2.9	7.4	114	48%	.334
2017	SLN	MLB	25	12	9	0	30	30	165²	170	17	3.0	8.6	158	50%	.327
2018	SLN	MLB	26	8	2	0	15	15	84¹	68	9	3.8	7.6	71	47%	.249
2019	SLN	MLB	27	7	6	0	21	21	105	98	11	3.2	8.3	96	46%	.292

Breakout: 23%   Improve: 54%   Collapse: 27%   Attrition: 10%   MLB: 97%
Comparables: Julio Teheran, Mat Latos, John Danks

Every injury-prone pitcher seems to go from "good when healthy" to "never quite healthy." Wacha has never offered guaranteed durability, but he posted a cFIP between 85 and 97 in each season from 2013 through 2017. In 2018, he finally wobbled off that tightrope, with a cFIP of 102 that suggests he was a below-average pitcher for the first time. That was, in no small part, because his stuff went backward even more than it had stepped forward in 2017. By cutting it loose for a year, Wacha seems to have permanently left something on the Busch Stadium mound. Though he's still young, the injury markers have gone from yellow flags to red ones, and he no longer looks like an ace in the making.

YEAR	TEAM	LVL	AGE	WHIP	ERA	DRA	WARP	MPH	FB%	WHF	CSP
2016	SLN	MLB	24	1.48	5.09	4.38	1.5	96.3	52.9	9	48
2017	SLN	MLB	25	1.36	4.13	3.83	3.2	97.2	52.8	10.9	49.9
2018	SLN	MLB	26	1.23	3.20	3.98	1.3	95.8	43.1	10.4	46.2
2019	SLN	MLB	27	1.28	3.80	4.21	1.0	96.1	50.6	10.4	48.5

Michael Wacha, continued

Pitch Shape vs LHH

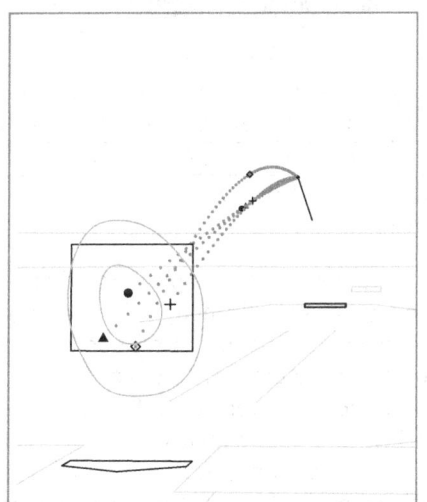

Pitch Shape vs RHH

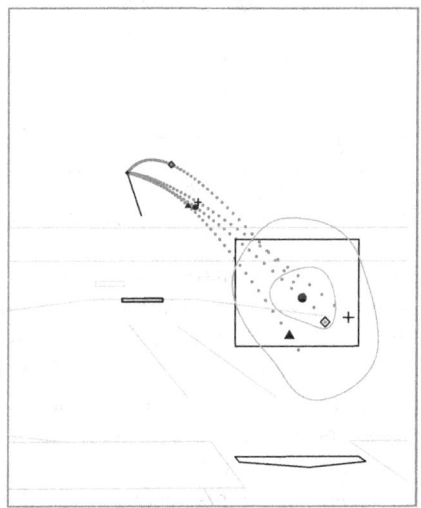

Type	Frequency	Velocity	H Movement	V Movement
● Fastball	41.7%	94.2 [106]	-6 [103]	-11.9 [112]
☐ Sinker	1.3%	94.3 [109]	-8 [138]	-13.7 [122]
+ Cutter	19.8%	89.9 [107]	3 [106]	-20.5 [113]
▲ Changeup	22.2%	86.6 [105]	-9.4 [110]	-23.4 [112]
✕ Splitter				
▽ Slider				
◇ Curveball	15.0%	76.4 [92]	7.5 [98]	-54.7 [85]
⊕ Slow Curveball				
✷ Knuckleball				
▼ Screwball				

Adam Wainwright   RHP

Born: 08/30/81   Age: 37   Bats: R   Throws: R
Height: 6'7"   Weight: 235   Origin: Round 1, 2000 Draft (#29 overall)

YEAR	TEAM	LVL	AGE	W	L	SV	G	GS	IP	H	HR	BB/9	K/9	K	GB%	BABIP
2016	SLN	MLB	34	13	9	0	33	33	198[2]	220	22	2.7	7.3	161	45%	.330
2017	SLN	MLB	35	12	5	0	24	23	123[1]	140	14	3.3	7.0	96	50%	.326
2018	SFD	AA	36	1	0	0	3	3	10	5	0	0.0	8.1	9	42%	.192
2018	SLN	MLB	36	2	4	0	8	8	40[1]	41	5	4.0	8.9	40	51%	.310
2019	SLN	MLB	37	7	7	0	40	19	117	115	12	3.4	7.8	101	46%	.300

Breakout: 10%   Improve: 46%   Collapse: 20%   Attrition: 13%   MLB: 87%
Comparables: Hiroki Kuroda, Jorge De La Rosa, Rick Reuschel

Over the last two years, Wainwright's career has been on life support multiple times. In what is increasingly a young man's game, he's distinctly old, with both the speed and the movement on his stuff fading fast. And yet, he's found his way to a very modern revelation: that throwing his best pitch more often can keep him afloat. He threw his famous, nostalgia-inducing curveball nearly 40 percent of the time, more than any other pitch. Wainwright is mostly curve-cutter-sinker these days, which is the optimal three-pitch mix if your goal is to keep batters from swinging aggressively. Despite the flattening stuff, he's getting just enough whiffs to get by, limiting opponents' power, and finessing his way to unlikely success, where success is defined as survival.

YEAR	TEAM	LVL	AGE	WHIP	ERA	DRA	WARP	MPH	FB%	WHF	CSP
2016	SLN	MLB	34	1.40	4.62	4.26	2.5	93.2	41.5	8.8	46.4
2017	SLN	MLB	35	1.50	5.11	4.84	1.0	92.2	46.8	7.8	47.5
2018	SFD	AA	36	0.50	0.00	4.56	0.1				
2018	SLN	MLB	36	1.46	4.46	3.78	0.7	91.6	38	9.6	45.5
2019	SLN	MLB	37	1.36	4.03	4.45	0.8	91.2	41.9	8.3	45.3

Adam Wainwright, continued

Pitch Shape vs LHH

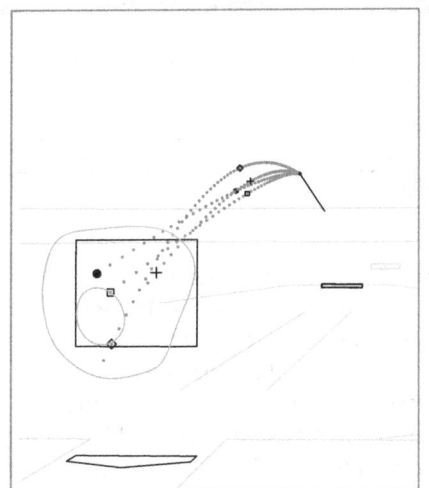

Pitch Shape vs RHH

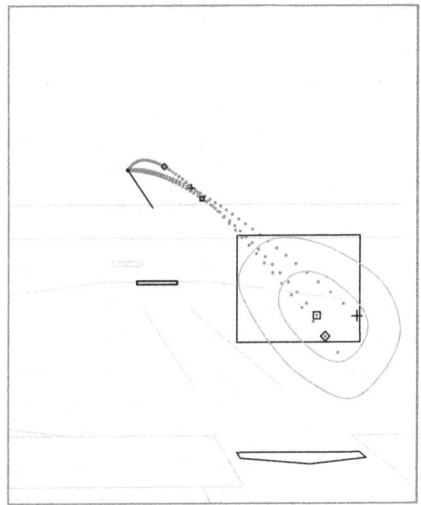

Type	Frequency	Velocity	H Movement	V Movement
● Fastball	12.3%	89.7 [91]	-4.4 [110]	-18.5 [91]
☐ Sinker	25.6%	90 [88]	-12.3 [103]	-22.5 [93]
+ Cutter	21.1%	84.5 [74]	5.7 [123]	-28.1 [83]
▲ Changeup	4.1%	81.1 [83]	-13.4 [89]	-32.4 [85]
✕ Splitter				
▽ Slider				
◇ Curveball	36.8%	73.9 [83]	17.4 [140]	-57.9 [78]
✦ Slow Curveball				
✶ Knuckleball				
▼ Screwball				

Randy Arozarena LF

Born: 02/28/95 Age: 24 Bats: R Throws: R
Height: 5'11" Weight: 170 Origin: International Free Agent, 2016

YEAR	TEAM	LVL	AGE	PA	R	2B	3B	HR	RBI	BB	K	SB	CS	AVG/OBP/SLG
2017	PMB	A+	22	295	38	22	3	8	40	13	53	10	4	.275/.333/.472
2017	SFD	AA	22	195	34	10	1	3	9	27	34	8	3	.252/.366/.380
2018	SFD	AA	23	102	22	5	0	7	21	6	25	9	3	.396/.455/.681
2018	MEM	AAA	23	311	42	16	0	5	28	28	59	17	5	.232/.328/.348
2019	SLN	MLB	24	251	32	10	1	7	23	18	63	9	3	.218/.290/.355

Breakout: 10% Improve: 27% Collapse: 5% Attrition: 21% MLB: 46%
Comparables: Austin Slater, Chad Huffman, Alex Hassan

There's more strength to Arozarena, from the hands and wrists up through the shoulders and down into his legs, than in most players of his size. It's not translating into consistent or intimidating power, however, and the way his swing works, it might not ever do so. As he's not ever likely to become a viable everyday center fielder, that puts real pressure on Arozarena's pure hit tool. His approach is polished, though he's still learning to adjust at the incredibly rapid pace the upper levels of professional baseball require. With plenty of speed and arm for either corner, he will get numerous chances to carve out a role, but without a studied change to that swing to generate more natural pop, it might be a strictly complementary one.

YEAR	TEAM	LVL	AGE	PA	DRC+	VORP	BABIP	BRR	FRAA	WARP
2017	PMB	A+	22	295	137	23.4	.313	-2.5	LF(47): 4.3, CF(13): -0.5	1.5
2017	SFD	AA	22	195	112	8.2	.299	2.7	LF(40): 0.1, CF(4): -0.9	0.5
2018	SFD	AA	23	102	193	15.4	.492	1.0	RF(12): 1.6, CF(6): -0.4	1.3
2018	MEM	AAA	23	311	82	9.3	.278	0.8	LF(49): -2.7, RF(18): 0.2	-0.5
2019	SLN	MLB	24	251	81	2.2	.271	0.5	LF 0, RF 0	0.1

Dylan Carlson   CF

Born: 10/23/98   Age: 20   Bats: B   Throws: L
Height: 6'3"   Weight: 195   Origin: Round 1, 2016 Draft (#33 overall)

YEAR	TEAM	LVL	AGE	PA	R	2B	3B	HR	RBI	BB	K	SB	CS	AVG/OBP/SLG
2016	CRD	RK	17	201	30	13	3	3	22	16	52	4	2	.251/.313/.404
2017	PEO	A	18	451	63	18	1	7	42	52	116	6	6	.240/.342/.347
2018	PEO	A	19	57	5	3	0	2	9	10	10	2	0	.234/.368/.426
2018	PMB	A+	19	441	63	19	3	9	53	52	78	6	3	.247/.345/.386
2019	SLN	MLB	20	251	19	7	0	6	24	16	76	0	0	.153/.211/.267

Breakout: 9%   Improve: 11%   Collapse: 0%   Attrition: 5%   MLB: 11%
Comparables: Nomar Mazara, Caleb Gindl, Jesse Winker

Calling 31 extra-base hits in 441 plate appearances a minor power breakout correctly (if modestly) characterizes Carlson's profile. He invites projection. Sure, he barely cracked double digits in the home run column in 2018, but he did it as a teenager, in the pitcher-friendly Midwest and Florida State Leagues. He controlled the strike zone, handled velocity well, and showed good instincts on the bases. His hit tool has to jump up to the other side of average in order for his potential to become production, but Carlson has all kinds of time, a build that really allows you to dream on the power, and the eternal platoon advantage.

YEAR	TEAM	LVL	AGE	PA	DRC+	VORP	BABIP	BRR	FRAA	WARP
2016	CRD	RK	17	201	113	1.2	.333	-1.6	CF(41): 6.5, LF(9): 0.2	0.6
2017	PEO	A	18	451	99	14.2	.323	2.6	RF(79): 0.8, CF(24): 0.1	0.7
2018	PEO	A	19	57	135	1.4	.257	-0.7	RF(10): 2.3, CF(4): -0.3	0.4
2018	PMB	A+	19	441	113	18.3	.286	1.7	RF(50): 4.7, LF(37): -0.1	1.2
2019	SLN	MLB	20	251	25	-16.1	.191	-0.5	RF -1, LF 1	-1.7

Adolis Garcia   RF
Born: 03/02/93   Age: 26   Bats: R   Throws: R
Height: 6'1"   Weight: 180   Origin: International Free Agent, 2017

YEAR	TEAM	LVL	AGE	PA	R	2B	3B	HR	RBI	BB	K	SB	CS	AVG/OBP/SLG
2017	SFD	AA	24	342	43	23	0	12	55	26	77	12	8	.285/.339/.476
2017	MEM	AAA	24	147	21	11	2	3	10	7	31	3	1	.301/.342/.478
2018	MEM	AAA	25	428	62	25	4	22	71	14	99	10	3	.256/.281/.500
2018	SLN	MLB	25	17	3	1	0	0	1	0	7	0	0	.118/.118/.176
2019	SLN	MLB	26	126	16	7	1	5	14	4	33	2	1	.233/.262/.433

Breakout: 6%   Improve: 18%   Collapse: 6%   Attrition: 17%   MLB: 34%
Comparables: Carlos Moncrief, Ray Sadler, Josh Kroeger

There's a chance that the single biggest play of the season, in the entire National League, came when the strapping and athletic Garcia came tearing around third base after a throwing error late in a game against the Brewers in late September. He was sure to score the tying run, all the way from first base—until he fell hilariously onto his belly about halfway between third and home. He got up, obviously flustered, and ran right into a waiting catcher's mitt. That's where he is right now. His tools and physical profile are thoroughly impressive. He has plus power, plus speed, a plus arm, and a feel for contact. He has zero feel for the strike zone, the base paths, or the outfield. The latter takes most of the fun out of the former.

YEAR	TEAM	LVL	AGE	PA	DRC+	VORP	BABIP	BRR	FRAA	WARP
2017	SFD	AA	24	342	119	18.6	.338	0.3	RF(73): 10.2, CF(10): 2.7	2.0
2017	MEM	AAA	24	147	105	9.5	.369	1.9	RF(24): 0.6, CF(10): 1.9	0.7
2018	MEM	AAA	25	428	88	15.9	.283	-0.1	RF(95): 11.4, CF(6): -0.1	1.1
2018	SLN	MLB	25	17	69	-2.7	.200	-0.4	RF(7): -0.4, LF(4): -0.1	-0.1
2019	SLN	MLB	26	126	80	1.3	.265	0.1	CF 0, LF 0	0.2

Nolan Gorman 3B

Born: 05/10/00 Age: 19 Bats: L Throws: R
Height: 6'1" Weight: 210 Origin: Round 1, 2018 Draft (#19 overall)

YEAR	TEAM	LVL	AGE	PA	R	2B	3B	HR	RBI	BB	K	SB	CS	AVG/OBP/SLG
2018	JCY	RK	18	167	41	10	1	11	28	24	37	1	3	.350/.443/.664
2018	PEO	A	18	107	8	3	0	6	16	10	39	0	2	.202/.280/.426
2019	SLN	MLB	19	251	26	6	0	12	28	13	97	0	0	.144/.187/.319

Breakout: 7% Improve: 9% Collapse: 0% Attrition: 4% MLB: 12%
Comparables: Rafael Devers, Domingo Santana, Nomar Mazara

Commendably, the Cardinals pushed their top pick in the 2018 Draft as far as failure would let him get over the summer. He demolished Rookie-level competition, but more than that, he showed total control of the game—of the barrel of his bat, of his glove and throwing arm, everything. As a young 18-year-old in full-season ball, Gorman saw the game speed up some, and learned a few lessons the hard way. There are real holes in his swing, or else his combination of left-handed power and athletic prowess to suit third base wouldn't have fallen to St. Louis in June. He refused to be overmatched, though, and showed enough power even in Peoria to really get scouts excited for 2019.

YEAR	TEAM	LVL	AGE	PA	DRC+	VORP	BABIP	BRR	FRAA	WARP
2018	JCY	RK	18	167	210	25.2	.411	-0.7	3B(33): 7.6	2.2
2018	PEO	A	18	107	77	2.3	.255	-0.5	3B(25): 3.9	0.3
2019	SLN	MLB	19	251	33	-15.0	.172	-0.6	3B 5	-1.1

Andrew Knizner C

Born: 02/03/95 Age: 24 Bats: R Throws: R
Height: 6'1" Weight: 200 Origin: Round 7, 2016 Draft (#226 overall)

YEAR	TEAM	LVL	AGE	PA	R	2B	3B	HR	RBI	BB	K	SB	CS	AVG/OBP/SLG
2016	JCY	RK	21	222	35	12	1	6	42	21	21	0	0	.319/.423/.492
2017	PEO	A	22	191	18	10	1	8	29	9	22	1	1	.279/.325/.480
2017	SFD	AA	22	202	27	13	0	4	22	14	27	0	1	.324/.371/.462
2018	SFD	AA	23	313	39	13	0	7	41	23	40	0	1	.313/.365/.434
2018	MEM	AAA	23	61	3	5	0	0	4	4	8	0	0	.315/.383/.407
2019	SLN	MLB	24	37	4	1	0	1	3	1	7	0	0	.229/.250/.343

Breakout: 16% Improve: 37% Collapse: 0% Attrition: 21% MLB: 54%
Comparables: Kevin Plawecki, J.T. Realmuto, Willson Contreras

Another converted collegiate infielder trying to figure it out behind the plate, Knizner has something other players in the same situation haven't often had: a bat that really could play most places on the diamond. There's not a great deal of power in his profile, but his hit tool is impressive, and he doesn't get himself out. He's knocking on the door of the Majors, but now the question will have to be asked: does MLB still open the door for players without a loud tool other than the ability to hit for average? If Knizner proves those gains in framing over a larger sample, that question will be moot.

YEAR	TEAM	P. COUNT	FRM RUNS	BLK RUNS	THRW RUNS	TOT RUNS
2017	SFD	6878	-3.0	0.0	0.2	-3.9
2018	MEM	2067	1.9	0.2	-0.1	1.9
2018	SFD	10157	-3.7	-1.9	-0.1	-6.0
2019	SLN	1353	-1.0	-0.2	-0.1	-1.3

YEAR	TEAM	LVL	AGE	PA	DRC+	VORP	BABIP	BRR	FRAA	WARP
2016	JCY	RK	21	222	179	18.3	.331	-0.1	C(21): -0.4, 1B(19): -0.9	1.2
2017	PEO	A	22	191	125	13.2	.282	0.5	C(26): -0.3, 1B(3): -0.1	0.9
2017	SFD	AA	22	202	141	17.7	.355	0.5	C(49): -3.5	1.0
2018	SFD	AA	23	313	133	21.9	.339	-1.4	C(74): -7.3	1.0
2018	MEM	AAA	23	61	116	3.8	.370	-0.1	C(16): 1.8	0.5
2019	SLN	MLB	24	37	68	0.2	.257	-0.1	C -2	-0.2

Elehuris Montero 3B

Born: 08/17/98 Age: 20 Bats: R Throws: R
Height: 6'3" Weight: 195 Origin: International Free Agent, 2014

YEAR	TEAM	LVL	AGE	PA	R	2B	3B	HR	RBI	BB	K	SB	CS	AVG/OBP/SLG
2016	DCA	RK	17	262	41	14	2	1	26	28	51	2	1	.260/.349/.352
2017	CRD	RK	18	208	30	16	1	5	36	22	33	0	2	.277/.370/.468
2018	PEO	A	19	425	68	28	3	15	69	33	81	2	0	.322/.381/.529
2018	PMB	A+	19	106	13	9	0	1	13	5	22	1	0	.286/.330/.408
2019	SLN	MLB	20	251	19	10	0	7	25	9	70	0	0	.163/.198/.290

Breakout: 13% Improve: 15% Collapse: 0% Attrition: 5% MLB: 15%
Comparables: Matt Dominguez, Rafael Devers, Matt Davidson

All that remains is some polishing. Montero has done enough over the last two years and demonstrated both his strengths and his weaknesses clearly enough that we don't have to wonder all that much about what kind of player he'll be. He's limited by a lack of overwhelming athleticism; he won't have great range at third or make plays with his legs. However, he's also blessed with a combination of power and bat-to-ball skill that could make him an elite right-handed hitter by the time he reaches the Majors. Montero's capable of hitting .300 and cranking 30 homers a year. He also has a great arm that helps make up for the lack of agility defensively. The open questions (his footwork at third and his approach at the plate) are all about aptitude, makeup, and neurology.

YEAR	TEAM	LVL	AGE	PA	DRC+	VORP	BABIP	BRR	FRAA	WARP
2016	DCA	RK	17	262	104	4.7	.328	0.5	3B(60): 2.6	0.9
2017	CRD	RK	18	208	140	10.3	.305	-0.5	3B(41): 2.8	0.8
2018	PEO	A	19	425	163	39.7	.372	0.3	3B(77): 2.7	4.0
2018	PMB	A+	19	106	117	5.7	.355	0.6	3B(20): 0.8	0.4
2019	SLN	MLB	20	251	28	-16.7	.195	-0.5	3B 1	-1.7

St. Louis Cardinals 2019

Malcom Nunez 3B
Born: 03/09/01   Age: 18   Bats: R   Throws: R
Height: 5'11"   Weight: 205   Origin: International Free Agent, 2018

YEAR	TEAM	LVL	AGE	PA	R	2B	3B	HR	RBI	BB	K	SB	CS	AVG/OBP/SLG
2018	DCA	RK	17	199	44	16	2	13	59	26	29	3	0	.415/.497/.774
2019	SLN	MLB	18	251	26	14	0	10	33	16	68	0	0	.221/.271/.414

Comparables: Adalberto Mondesi, Wilmer Flores, Tommy Brown

Nunez won the Dominican Summer League's Triple Crown in 2018 as a 17-year-old signee out of Cuba. "Won" doesn't do it justice: the teenager had the best offensive performance of any player in any system this year. He doesn't do it in an orthodox way, physically, but baseball history is littered with successful third basemen who neither played nor looked like most of their cohort. Already a name on the radar when he signed, Nunez vaulted himself into serious (if speculative) consideration as one of the game's better prospects at the hot corner. But perhaps best of all, however, is that because of improved international relations, Nunez didn't have to risk his life or his future to ply his trade, riding a raft or throwing his fate to a seedy agent. Not everything is better than it used to be, but at least one thing is.

YEAR	TEAM	LVL	AGE	PA	DRC+	VORP	BABIP	BRR	FRAA	WARP
2018	DCA	RK	17	199	230	37.1	.437	0.5	3B(30): -1.0, 1B(5): 1.2	2.9
2019	SLN	MLB	18	251	82	-0.3	.262	-0.5	3B -1, 1B 0	-0.1

Delvin Perez SS

Born: 11/24/98 Age: 20 Bats: R Throws: R
Height: 6'3" Weight: 175 Origin: Round 1, 2016 Draft (#23 overall)

YEAR	TEAM	LVL	AGE	PA	R	2B	3B	HR	RBI	BB	K	SB	CS	AVG/OBP/SLG
2016	CRD	RK	17	180	19	8	4	0	19	12	28	12	1	.294/.352/.393
2017	CRD	RK	18	50	7	1	2	0	5	5	10	2	1	.238/.320/.357
2017	JCY	RK	18	90	7	1	1	0	4	12	14	3	4	.184/.311/.224
2018	SCO	A-	19	269	22	5	3	1	21	28	54	8	6	.213/.301/.272
2019	SLN	MLB	20	251	19	2	0	5	16	10	73	2	1	.119/.153/.188

Breakout: 4% Improve: 4% Collapse: 0% Attrition: 1% MLB: 4%
Comparables: Tyler Wade, Rey Navarro, Amed Rosario

The Cardinals believe in Perez's talent—the tools that led them to bet on him when he tumbled down the 2016 Draft board. It's increasingly difficult, though, to reconcile the potential that faith implies with the lack of production or progress through three pro seasons. Perez's glove remains promising, though inconsistent. Banged for performance-enhancing drugs before the draft, he's hit just one pro homer in nearly 600 plate appearances. He's fast, but doesn't always run that way. He has a feel for the barrel, but often, none for the game. More than anything, though, Perez's greatest weakness is his strength, and if he can't build on that, he's going to need that line for job interviews soon.

YEAR	TEAM	LVL	AGE	PA	DRC+	VORP	BABIP	BRR	FRAA	WARP
2016	CRD	RK	17	180	141	15.1	.353	0.8	SS(40): -3.7, CF(1): -0.1	0.5
2017	CRD	RK	18	50	97	2.7	.294	1.6	SS(9): -1.1	0.1
2017	JCY	RK	18	90	75	2.0	.226	0.7	SS(22): -0.5	0.0
2018	SCO	A-	19	269	63	0.8	.272	-2.2	SS(64): 6.2	-0.2
2019	SLN	MLB	20	251	-12	-24.3	.145	-0.2	SS -1	-2.7

St. Louis Cardinals 2019

Ramon Urias   INF
Born: 06/03/94   Age: 25   Bats: R   Throws: R
Height: 5'10"   Weight: 150   Origin: International Free Agent, 2010

YEAR	TEAM	LVL	AGE	PA	R	2B	3B	HR	RBI	BB	K	SB	CS	AVG/OBP/SLG
2018	SFD	AA	24	194	28	19	0	8	27	18	29	1	2	.333/.406/.589
2018	MEM	AAA	24	149	20	9	0	5	17	6	29	0	0	.261/.291/.430
2019	SLN	MLB	25	37	4	2	0	1	4	2	8	0	0	.235/.278/.382

Breakout: 7%   Improve: 32%   Collapse: 8%   Attrition: 26%   MLB: 57%
Comparables: Joey Wendle, Taylor Featherston, David Bote

Things change slowly. We live, perhaps, in the Golden Age of diminutive sluggers, but there remains a strong and systemic bias in baseball scouting against players who seem dramatically undersized, even if they hit really well over a relatively long period. Urias embodies that as much as any player in baseball. He signed with the Rangers in 2010, but when he didn't immediately break out in the Dominican Summer League, he found himself on a five-year sojourn through the baseball wilderness that is the Mexican League. When the Cardinals plucked him out of there, he'd batted .320/.406/.469 in over 2,000 plate appearances, and in his first season Stateside, he hit .300 at the highest levels in the minors. A good enough glove to back up every infield spot, he's now a near-certain future big-leaguer.

YEAR	TEAM	LVL	AGE	PA	DRC+	VORP	BABIP	BRR	FRAA	WARP
2018	SFD	AA	24	194	182	20.4	.361	-1.8	2B(30): -1.7, SS(7): 1.2	1.6
2018	MEM	AAA	24	149	90	1.6	.296	-0.5	2B(18): 0.7, 3B(7): -1.0	-0.1
2019	SLN	MLB	25	37	71	-0.1	.288	-0.1	2B 0	0.0

Justin Williams RF

Born: 08/20/95 Age: 23 Bats: L Throws: R
Height: 6'2" Weight: 215 Origin: Round 2, 2013 Draft (#52 overall)

YEAR	TEAM	LVL	AGE	PA	R	2B	3B	HR	RBI	BB	K	SB	CS	AVG/OBP/SLG
2016	PCH	A+	20	203	23	11	0	4	31	6	26	0	1	.330/.350/.448
2016	MNT	AA	20	155	20	7	2	6	28	5	30	0	1	.250/.277/.446
2017	MNT	AA	21	409	53	21	3	14	72	37	69	6	2	.301/.364/.489
2018	TBA	MLB	22	1	0	0	0	0	0	0	0	0	0	.000/.000/.000
2018	DUR	AAA	22	386	41	18	0	8	46	25	81	4	3	.258/.313/.376
2018	MEM	AAA	22	76	8	3	0	3	11	5	17	0	1	.217/.276/.391
2019	SLN	MLB	23	251	24	10	1	8	30	11	58	1	1	.224/.263/.373

Breakout: 15%   Improve: 32%   Collapse: 1%   Attrition: 8%   MLB: 33%
Comparables: J.D. Martinez, Preston Tucker, Tyler Austin

The tools are tempting, but Williams keeps cobbling together frustrating seasons in which only part of his talent really shines through. He matriculated to the Majors in 2018 but got just a single plate appearance, and then was traded for the second time in four years. A capable defender in either outfield corner with a left-handed bat that seems as though it could bloom into either a powerful one or a consistent line-drive threat, he nonetheless struggles to put it all together. The physicality isn't getting better; it's time to see whether he can make the leap skills-wise.

YEAR	TEAM	LVL	AGE	PA	DRC+	VORP	BABIP	BRR	FRAA	WARP
2016	PCH	A+	20	203	139	8.5	.361	-3.3	RF(43): 3.5	0.7
2016	MNT	AA	20	155	87	3.7	.274	0.8	RF(34): -1.7	-0.3
2017	MNT	AA	21	409	141	18.7	.334	-2.0	RF(80): -4.8, LF(7): 1.2	1.2
2018	TBA	MLB	22	1	83	-0.5	.000	0.0	RF(1): 0.0	0.0
2018	DUR	AAA	22	386	97	-4.8	.315	-2.7	RF(80): 13.7, LF(2): 1.0	1.3
2018	MEM	AAA	22	76	86	-0.6	.240	-1.1	LF(10): 4.2, RF(7): 0.9	0.4
2019	SLN	MLB	23	251	72	-2.1	.261	-0.4	RF 1, LF 1	0.0

St. Louis Cardinals 2019

Genesis Cabrera LHP
Born: 10/10/96   Age: 22   Bats: L   Throws: L
Height: 6'1"   Weight: 170   Origin: International Free Agent, 2013

YEAR	TEAM	LVL	AGE	W	L	SV	G	GS	IP	H	HR	BB/9	K/9	K	GB%	BABIP
2016	BGR	A	19	11	5	0	23	22	116	110	9	3.7	7.4	96	36%	.305
2017	PCH	A+	20	4	5	0	13	12	69²	45	3	3.2	7.8	60	39%	.230
2017	MNT	AA	20	5	4	0	12	12	64²	75	6	3.8	7.1	51	37%	.332
2018	MNT	AA	21	7	6	0	21	20	113²	90	11	4.5	9.8	124	35%	.282
2018	SFD	AA	21	1	3	0	5	5	24²	24	3	4.7	7.7	21	37%	.300
2019	SLN	MLB	22	1	1	0	11	0	11¹	10	1	4.8	9.3	12	34%	.291

Breakout: 5%   Improve: 10%   Collapse: 4%   Attrition: 7%   MLB: 16%
Comparables: Chaz Roe, Alex Burnett, Touki Toussaint

If he ever gets bumped from a full-fledged rotation role, let's hope that Cabrera can at least be used as an opener. His arsenal feels like the start of something good. His arm is so loose and his delivery so naturally deceptive that his changeup has to improve only slightly from where it is. His heater can run into the high 90s, and his cutter-like slider can work to either side of the plate out of his high slot. Cabrera's ability to work to all quadrants will be crucial, given the interplay between his raw stuff and the angles at which he throws it, and therein lies the rub. Right now, his command might be ahead of his control, which is a very strange state of affairs. There's no guarantee he'll ever throw enough strikes, but if he can tuck just enough into the zone, the swings will come for the ones outside.

YEAR	TEAM	LVL	AGE	WHIP	ERA	DRA	WARP	MPH	FB%	WHF	CSP
2016	BGR	A	19	1.36	3.88	5.65	-0.9				
2017	PCH	A+	20	1.00	2.84	3.91	1.1				
2017	MNT	AA	20	1.58	3.62	4.28	0.7				
2018	MNT	AA	21	1.29	4.12	5.12	0.3				
2018	SFD	AA	21	1.50	4.74	5.21	0.0				
2019	SLN	MLB	22	1.39	4.50	4.78	0.0				

Seth Elledge RHP

Born: 05/20/96   Age: 23   Bats: R   Throws: R
Height: 6'3"   Weight: 230   Origin: Round 4, 2017 Draft (#123 overall)

YEAR	TEAM	LVL	AGE	W	L	SV	G	GS	IP	H	HR	BB/9	K/9	K	GB%	BABIP
2017	CLN	A	21	3	0	5	15	0	21	14	1	2.6	15.0	35	40%	.310
2018	MOD	A+	22	5	1	9	31	0	38^1	18	1	3.5	12.7	54	53%	.221
2018	SFD	AA	22	3	1	4	13	0	16^2	13	3	3.2	10.8	20	44%	.250
2019	SLN	MLB	23	2	1	2	39	0	41^1	32	4	4.4	10.7	49	42%	.299

Breakout: 7%   Improve: 8%   Collapse: 3%   Attrition: 7%   MLB: 18%
Comparables: Steve Geltz, David Robertson, Alejandro Chacin

A fourth-round college draftee in 2017, Elledge has shredded the minor leagues with a pretty simple mixture. He throws a mid-90s fastball and a slider to which he can add and subtract, and the shape of which he can adjust to suit the situation and matchup. He also has a usable changeup, but he's on the fast track now, and if Elledge can demonstrate the command and feel he's had to this point, he won't much need a third pitch. Developing it would just be icing on the cake, the kind of gear-shifter that could turn the strapping right-hander into the very model of the modern multi-inning relief weapon.

YEAR	TEAM	LVL	AGE	WHIP	ERA	DRA	WARP	MPH	FB%	WHF	CSP
2017	CLN	A	21	0.95	3.00	2.62	0.6				
2018	MOD	A+	22	0.86	1.17	3.18	0.8				
2018	SFD	AA	22	1.14	4.32	2.35	0.5				
2019	SLN	MLB	23	1.26	3.58	4.19	0.4				

Ryan Helsley RHP

Born: 07/18/94 Age: 24 Bats: R Throws: R
Height: 6'1" Weight: 195 Origin: Round 5, 2015 Draft (#161 overall)

YEAR	TEAM	LVL	AGE	W	L	SV	G	GS	IP	H	HR	BB/9	K/9	K	GB%	BABIP
2016	PEO	A	21	10	2	0	17	17	95	77	3	1.8	10.3	109	41%	.301
2017	PMB	A+	22	8	2	0	17	16	93²	72	3	2.9	8.7	91	44%	.277
2017	SFD	AA	22	3	1	0	6	6	33²	25	4	4.0	11.0	41	43%	.262
2018	SFD	AA	23	3	2	0	7	7	41	30	5	4.4	9.7	44	49%	.243
2018	MEM	AAA	23	2	1	0	5	5	26²	18	2	3.0	11.5	34	38%	.262
2019	SLN	MLB	24	1	0	0	11	0	11¹	9	1	3.6	9.8	12	40%	.290

Breakout: 14% Improve: 27% Collapse: 20% Attrition: 32% MLB: 58%
Comparables: Jake Arrieta, David Rollins, Austin Voth

After the United States government drove them from their ancestral homeland, legend says that three Cherokee elders were to meet to determine the location of their new capital city. As dusk drew near, however, one still failed to show, so the other two agreed to go ahead with their planning without him. "Ta'ligwu," a Cherokee word meaning "two is enough," became more than a motto when they named their new capital city Tahlequah. It now rests in northeastern Oklahoma, where Helsley was born and raised, where he went to college, and where the Cardinals found him and drafted him. He's an exceptional athlete with plus makeup, and a high-spin fastball-curve combo. In order to be a solid mid-rotation arm, in fact, he just needs to overcome the shoulder issues that slowed him in 2018 and to further develop his budding cutter. Two is rarely enough when it comes to starters' pitch selection.

YEAR	TEAM	LVL	AGE	WHIP	ERA	DRA	WARP	MPH	FB%	WHF	CSP
2016	PEO	A	21	1.01	1.61	2.46	3.0				
2017	PMB	A+	22	1.09	2.69	3.19	2.3				
2017	SFD	AA	22	1.19	2.67	2.93	0.9				
2018	SFD	AA	23	1.22	4.39	3.33	1.0				
2018	MEM	AAA	23	1.01	3.71	2.55	0.9				
2019	SLN	MLB	24	1.19	3.23	3.74	0.1				

Alex Reyes RHP

Born: 08/29/94 Age: 24 Bats: R Throws: R
Height: 6'3" Weight: 175 Origin: International Free Agent, 2012

YEAR	TEAM	LVL	AGE	W	L	SV	G	GS	IP	H	HR	BB/9	K/9	K	GB%	BABIP
2016	MEM	AAA	21	2	3	0	14	14	65^1	63	6	4.4	12.8	93	42%	.365
2016	SLN	MLB	21	4	1	1	12	5	46	33	1	4.5	10.2	52	44%	.283
2018	SLN	MLB	23	0	0	0	1	1	4	3	0	4.5	4.5	2	40%	.300
2019	SLN	MLB	24	6	4	0	16	16	84	65	6	3.8	11.4	108	40%	.296

Breakout: 26% Improve: 57% Collapse: 14% Attrition: 20% MLB: 86%
Comparables: Tyler Glasnow, Matt Harvey, Jordan Walden

In this age of desensitization to tragedies and trials, Tommy John surgery ranks right up there with skin cancer and global climate change among things that should be taken more seriously. When Reyes had his in early 2017, many observers shrugged it off, figuring he'd be back by the middle of 2018, ready to take his place at the front of the Cardinals' rotation. He kind of, sort of, almost was, but during his rehab stint, he felt something start to go wrong in the back of his shoulder. Wanting to make it back to the majors and be categorized as a big-leaguer if he again hit the DL, he pitched through it. After just one truncated start, he was shelved for the season, and his star has dimmed deeply now. Blame Reyes for not being forthright, but save plenty of venom for the people who have allowed such a disparity to develop between the treatment and pay of major and minor leaguers, and spare not the people who foolhardily underestimated the risk of injury his extreme velocity and mechanics posed. Most importantly, remember: TINSTAAPP.

YEAR	TEAM	LVL	AGE	WHIP	ERA	DRA	WARP	MPH	FB%	WHF	CSP
2016	MEM	AAA	21	1.45	4.96	3.01	1.7				
2016	SLN	MLB	21	1.22	1.57	3.45	0.9	100.1	63.9	12.4	45.8
2018	SLN	MLB	23	1.25	0.00	8.15	-0.1	97.2	57.5	4.1	43
2019	SLN	MLB	24	1.19	2.86	3.17	1.9	99.5	64.9	11.6	45.4

St. Louis Cardinals 2019

Griffin Roberts   RHP
Born: 06/13/96   Age: 23   Bats: R   Throws: R
Height: 6'3"   Weight: 205   Origin: Round 1, 2018 Draft (#43 overall)

YEAR	TEAM	LVL	AGE	W	L	SV	G	GS	IP	H	HR	BB/9	K/9	K	GB%	BABIP
2018	CRD	RK	22	0	1	1	7	2	8²	6	0	4.2	11.4	11	55%	.300
2019	SLN	MLB	23	2	1	1	22	2	31²	31	3	7.5	8.0	28	47%	.312

Comparables: Tanner Anderson, Gerardo Concepcion, Matthew Carasiti

Roberts spent his days at Wake Forest dekein' ACC hitters with a demonic slider, perhaps the best in the 2018 draft class. It's a two-plane problem of a pitch, off a fastball that sits comfortably in the mid-90s and can ramp up to 97 or 98 miles per hour in short bursts. For some of his collegiate career, Roberts closed, and he could be ticketed for that role again in the future, but his size and his ability to repeat his release point provide some reason to believe he can start. No longer is leaning heavily on a slider, even making it the primary weapon in one's arsenal, disqualifying for a would-be starter, and Roberts is a great example. He just needs to more consistently fade his changeup out of the lane of his heater.

YEAR	TEAM	LVL	AGE	WHIP	ERA	DRA	WARP	MPH	FB%	WHF	CSP
2018	CRD	RK	22	1.15	6.23	3.43	0.2				
2019	SLN	MLB	23	1.79	5.60	6.54	-0.5				

LINEOUTS

Hitters

HITTER	POS	TEAM	LVL	AGE	PA	R	2B	3B	HR	RBI	BB	K	SB	CS	AVG/OBP/SLG	DRC+	WARP
Luken Baker	1B	CRD	Rk	21	28	10	2	0	1	7	3	4	0	0	.500/.536/.708	213	0.2
	1B	PEO	A	21	156	16	9	0	3	15	16	31	0	0	.288/.359/.417	144	0.6
Conner Capel	CF	LYN	A+	21	383	47	17	3	6	44	49	72	15	10	.261/.355/.388	110	0.7
	CF	PMB	A+	21	126	11	6	1	1	19	7	30	0	1	.248/.296/.342	81	-0.4
Ivan Herrera	C	CRD	Rk	18	130	23	6	4	1	25	11	20	1	1	.348/.423/.500	154	0.6
Joe Hudson	C	LOU	AAA	27	60	5	3	0	0	3	8	15	0	0	.235/.339/.294	90	0.3
	C	MOB	AA	27	28	2	1	1	1	5	1	7	0	0	.346/.393/.577	120	0.1
	C	SLC	AAA	27	101	13	6	0	3	14	10	18	0	0	.311/.380/.478	123	0.7
	C	ANA	MLB	27	12	0	1	0	0	1	0	0	0	0	.167/.167/.250	93	0.1
Jonatan Machado	OF	PEO	A	19	96	8	4	0	0	8	3	15	3	2	.185/.208/.228	38	-1.2
	OF	JCY	Rk	19	214	30	10	0	2	21	17	41	9	5	.292/.355/.375	95	-0.4
	OF	SCO	A-	19	46	2	0	0	0	2	3	15	0	0	.048/.109/.048	-12	-0.4
Francisco Pena	C	SLN	MLB	28	142	10	3	0	2	8	6	43	1	0	.203/.239/.271	54	-0.8
Max Schrock	INF	MEM	AAA	23	457	41	22	0	4	42	24	36	10	5	.249/.296/.331	72	-1.1
Edmundo Sosa	SS	SFD	AA	22	279	34	17	1	7	32	9	52	1	2	.276/.308/.429	92	-0.2
	SS	MEM	AAA	22	209	31	13	0	5	27	13	42	5	2	.262/.321/.408	89	0.4
	SS	SLN	MLB	22	3	1	0	0	0	0	1	1	0	0	.000/.333/.000	84	0.0
Wadye Ynfante	CF	SCO	A-	20	286	33	15	1	4	25	21	101	10	5	.213/.301/.328	63	-0.1

Luken Baker is tall and bats right-handed, so he can't be Dan Vogelbach's secret twin, but he *might* be his accidentally-unleashed funhouse mirror reflection. ⓧ It's tempting to dream on an everyday future for a toolsy left-handed batter, but guys like **Conner Capel** nearly always see half those tools fade and end up as either a platoon bat or a fourth outfielder. ⓧ Panamanian backstop **Ivan Herrera** has a chance to catch some helium this summer, as he moves beyond the complex leagues at age 19. ⓧ **Joe Hudson** was great as the police chief on *Hill Street Blues*, and less so as a major league catcher for a few weeks. ⓧ Youth and speed are on his side, but as it stands, **Jonatan Machado** is about 30 pounds and two power grades away from being a viable regular even in center field. ⓧ **Francisco Pena** has catching in his blood, and teammates love him; between those things and his offensive skills, he's qualified to be a fine quality control coach. ⓧ The only way diminutive, modestly athletic **Max Schrock** was going to carve out a big-league career of any import was to keep hitting for average, and when he reached Triple-A, he stopped doing that. ⓧ His modest, developing pop befits the smooth defensive shortstop he projected to be, but **Edmundo Sosa** looks more like a utility infielder instead. ⓧ He's got the quirky name and the single-tool profile (it's plus speed; the rest is hopes and prayers) of a prospect who never makes it, but there's still time for **Wadye Ynfante** to surprise us.

St. Louis Cardinals 2019

Pitchers

PITCHER	TEAM	LVL	AGE	W	L	SV	G	GS	IP	H	HR	BB/9	K/9	K	GB%	WHIP	ERA	DRA	WARP
Brett Cecil	SLN	MLB	31	1	1	0	40	0	32^2	39	5	6.9	5.2	19	41%	1.96	6.89	8.61	-1.4
Junior Fernandez	PMB	A+	21	1	0	3	8	0	9^2	9	0	1.9	6.5	7	43%	1.14	0.00	3.28	0.2
	SFD	AA	21	0	0	0	16	0	21	19	1	6.9	7.3	17	36%	1.67	5.14	4.64	0.1
Giovanny Gallegos	NYA	MLB	26	0	0	1	4	0	10	10	2	2.7	9.0	10	41%	1.30	4.50	5.38	-0.1
	SWB	AAA	26	2	1	2	17	0	27^2	24	1	2.3	13.3	41	39%	1.12	3.90	2.03	1.0
	MEM	AAA	26	0	0	1	13	0	16^2	7	0	1.6	8.6	16	45%	0.60	0.54	2.55	0.5
	SLN	MLB	26	0	0	0	2	0	1^1	1	0	0.0	13.5	2	0%	0.75	0.00	6.81	0.0
Derian Gonzalez	MEM	AAA	23	0	0	1	8	0	10^2	13	0	3.4	10.1	12	44%	1.59	5.91	2.59	0.3
	SFD	AA	23	4	0	1	13	0	16^1	13	0	3.9	5.5	10	58%	1.22	2.76	4.40	0.1
Mike Mayers	MEM	AAA	26	0	0	3	5	0	7^2	5	0	4.7	9.4	8	57%	1.17	0.00	3.42	0.1
	SLN	MLB	26	2	1	1	50	0	51^2	59	7	2.6	8.5	49	44%	1.43	4.70	4.06	0.5
Ryan Meisinger	BOW	AA	24	0	0	0	11	0	18^1	22	4	2.5	9.3	19	54%	1.47	4.42	2.53	0.5
	NOR	AAA	24	2	0	1	21	0	27^2	21	1	3.3	11.7	36	41%	1.12	2.28	2.71	0.8
	BAL	MLB	24	2	1	0	18	1	21	18	6	4.3	9.0	21	34%	1.33	6.43	7.30	-0.6
Johan Oviedo	PEO	A	20	10	10	1	25	23	121^2	108	6	5.8	8.7	118	38%	1.54	4.22	4.30	1.2
Tyler Webb	SDN	MLB	27	0	1	0	4	0	5	6	2	5.4	7.2	4	41%	1.80	12.60	8.27	-0.2
	ELP	AAA	27	1	1	0	19	0	22	20	1	3.3	11.5	28	38%	1.27	2.05	2.87	0.6
	MEM	AAA	27	0	0	0	11	1	19^2	9	1	1.8	9.6	21	41%	0.66	2.29	3.24	0.4
	SLN	MLB	27	0	0	0	18	0	15^1	16	1	3.5	6.5	11	31%	1.43	1.76	6.76	-0.3
Jake Woodford	SFD	AA	21	3	8	0	16	16	81	94	13	3.9	6.2	56	48%	1.59	5.22	4.77	0.5
	MEM	AAA	21	5	5	0	12	12	64	64	5	3.8	6.3	45	38%	1.42	4.50	4.92	0.5

No pitcher who tossed at least 30 innings in 2018 had a worse cFIP than The Man With Two Middle Names, **Brett Cecil**. ⓧ A fastball with triple-digit heat won't save **Junior Fernandez** until he finds his way clear to bring his walk percentage down into single digits. ⓧ His age and thin arsenal make **Giovanny Gallegos** easy to overlook, but his track record of success and missing bats makes him easy to dream on. ⓧ Brunette **Steven Gingery** has a fresh Tommy John scar, good fastball command, and a changeup more deceptive than his surname, which is a good start. ⓧ If he can stay on the mound long enough to establish his feel for them, **Derian Gonzalez** should ride two average-plus secondary offerings (a change and a hook) to a solid bullpen career. ⓧ Throwing 97 now, apparently, and having added four miles per hour to his slider from March to September of 2018, **Mike Mayers** has become a wild but effective relief option. ⓧ **Ryan Meisinger**, a Maryland native, rose quickly through the Orioles system after being drafted in 2015 and made his MLB debut this season, which was a cool moment. Less cool: Meisinger got torched by the long ball, surrendering homers in over half of his first 11 appearances. ⚾ Tall and blessed with a plus fastball, **Johan Oviedo** is still getting just this passing mention, which is a clue about where the rest of his arsenal and his command profile stand. ⚾ Strapping lefty **Tyler Webb** has the stuff to rack up strikeouts in the Majors, and the inconsistency to rack up six weeks a year of vacation, in the form of DFA limbo. ⚾ Former first-round pick **Jake Woodford** has good control and a heavy fastball, but there's nothing in his arsenal that misses bats, or even the barrels of them.

Cardinals Prospects

The State of the System:
The Cardinals system has thinned out significantly in recent years, due to graduations and trades, but who knows what plus regular lurks in the lair where Devil Magic is conjured.

The Top Ten:

1 **Alex Reyes   RHP**　　　　　OFP: 70   Likely: 60   ETA: Debuted in 2016
Born: 08/29/94   Age: 24   Bats: R   Throws: R   Height: 6'3"   Weight: 175
Origin: International Free Agent, 2012

The Report: After missing all of 2017 due to Tommy John surgery, it looked like all systems were go for Reyes at the beginning of 2018. The "number-one-prospect-in-baseball" stuff was back and accounted for on rehab. His 2018 MLB debut in May looked fine, despite command issues that aren't uncommon for a pitcher coming off Tommy John. Reyes was then immediately shut down afterwards with a torn lat. He's only 24, and still has potentially the best stuff among all prospect arms, but man we are going to need to see it on the field at some point. The Cardinals might be best served easing him in as a reliever in 2019. That also might be his long term role now.

　The Risks: Medium. On the one hand Reyes is literally as "major-league ready" as one can be while maintaining eligibility for a prospect list. On the other, he has functionally missed two full seasons. The lat injury isn't super concerning in and of itself but the larger pattern very much is.

　Ben Carsley's Fantasy Take: Honestly, there isn't any one way to value (or devalue) Reyes at this point. If you think he's still a top-10 prospect because of his upside as a starter, I totally get it. If you think he's only a top-50 guy at this point thanks to the injuries and reliever risk, that's fair, too. Personally, I'm hedging my bets a bit and will probably have him somewhere in the 15-to-25 range. To each his own. Good luck if you own him!

2 **Nolan Gorman   3B**　　　　　OFP: 70   Likely: 55   ETA: 2022
Born: 05/10/00   Age: 19   Bats: L   Throws: R   Height: 6'1"   Weight: 210
Origin: Round 1, 2018 Draft (#19 overall)

The Report: Gorman slid down draft rankings his senior season due to concerns about his hit tool and ultimate defensive home, but the bat sure looked fine in his pro debut. Gorman mashed 17 home runs in 63 games between the Appy and Midwest Leagues and it's not a small sample fluke, as he arguably had the biggest raw power in his draft class. The swing has some stiffness to it, but Gorman has a strong approach for an 18-year-old and should get most of his plus-plus raw power into games. I hate comps, but something like 2017-18 Travis Shaw could be a fair approximation of his bat at peak. Gorman isn't Travis Shaw with the glove though—there's a sentence I never thought I'd type—and there are concerns he might have to move off third base. He's not all that rangy at the hot corner and his arm is only "sufficient."

The Risks: Extreme. There are hit tool issues, perhaps positional ones, and his first taste of full-season ball came with a lot of swing-and-miss.

Ben Carsley's Fantasy Take: Gorman just ranked fifth on Bret Sayre's list of top-50 dynasty league signees from 2018, but he'd be third on my list. I love the power potential and the organizational fit, and those of you who've been along on this ride with me for a few years now won't be shocked that I'm willing to overlook the swing-and-miss to a certain extent. Gorman is a borderline top-50 overall prospect for me already, and he's the type of guy who we could all value the same way we look at Austin Riley right now in a year or two.

3. Dakota Hudson   RHP

OFP: 60   Likely: 50   ETA: Debuted in 2018
Born: 09/15/94   Age: 24   Bats: R   Throws: R   Height: 6'5"   Weight: 215
Origin: Round 1, 2016 Draft (#34 overall)

The Report: As mentioned above, the Cardinals like to debut their starting pitching prospects in the bullpen, but Hudson might be there to stay after showing off a dominant three-pitch mix in his two-month major-league trial. His fastball sits 96-98 with arm-side dive from the two-seamer; the occasional four-seamers show some cut. His cutter is more like a 92 mph slider and it can be patently unfair. His actual slider is the change of pace offering, as it sits in the mid-80s and features more cut that tilt. That doesn't make a lot of sense, but it works. He's shown a curve and change as a starter, but they lag behind and he works best as a three-pitch reliever. Hudson has struggled to harness his repertoire at times, but it's closer stuff, and this may end up more of a Trevor Rosenthal situation than a Carlos Martinez one.

The Risks: Low. He needs to clean up the control and command, but Hudson is ready to be an impact arm in the majors.

Ben Carsley's Fantasy Take: Hudson is a decent add for those of you who are hunting for saves in deep leagues, as he could have a good enough strikeout rate and WHIP to be worth rostering even if he's not closing. He may be the rare reliever who's good enough to sneak onto the back of the top-200 thanks in part his proximity to the majors and the relatively clearish path to closing time in St. Louis.

4. Andrew Knizner   C

OFP: 55   Likely: 45   ETA: September 2019
Born: 02/03/95   Age: 24   Bats: R   Throws: R   Height: 6'1"   Weight: 200
Origin: Round 7, 2016 Draft (#226 overall)

The Report: Knizner actually has a pretty fun set of offensive tools. He has an excellent catcher's build and there's almost no extra weight on the frame. He has fair quick twitch movements and reacts well both offensively and defensively.

Knizner knows how to hit. He has plus bat speed, excellent weight transfer, a compact swing, and plus hand-eye that allows him to make solid contact around the field. He has a tendency to expand the zone, especially mid-late in counts, and he could benefit from more discipline. He has above-average raw power, but his compact swing and a penchant for going the other way suggests he'll have below-average in-game power. An adjustment to hit the ball out front more could potentially unlock another tier of offensive output.

It's less pretty behind the plate, as Knizner is a below-average receiver. He tends to stab a bit at pitches low in the zone and often won't get calls there. His arm is below-average and even though he can make up for it a bit with his quick transition and good footwork, he'll likely be fringe-average at controlling the run game and decline from there as he ages. He blocks balls well and won't give up too many passed balls, for what it's worth.

The Risks: Low. Outside of the makeup and hit tool, there's just not a ton to add value to the profile. As an offense-first catcher, there's a real chance he won't hit for enough power and get on base enough to start. He is a catcher who can hit though, so overall the risk that he won't at least be able to perform as a bench player is low.

Ben Carsley's Fantasy Take: Knizner may be an intriguing fantasy option down the line if and when he gets regular playing time. But between the fact that all catching prospects are just designed to hurt us and the odds that Knizner ends up as nothing more than a backup, he's not a guy dynasty leaguers need to worry about unless your league rosters 200-plus prospects.

5. Elehuris Montero   3B

OFP: 55   Likely: 45   ETA: 2021
Born: 08/17/98   Age: 20   Bats: R   Throws: R   Height: 6'3"   Weight: 195
Origin: International Free Agent, 2014

The Report: Relatively unknown outside of prospecting circles, Montero enjoyed a breakout 2018 season. As a teenager, he torched Midwest League pitching to the tune of .322/.381/.522, earning a late season promotion to Palm Beach. He was arguably one of the most advanced bats in the league, featuring a quiet swing and a knack for barrelling the ball. Montero also shows an approach not often seen in someone so young, handling velocity well and rarely getting fooled on secondaries. There is power in his game as well, generated by his natural strength and a swing path that gets leverage.

In the field, Montero is not going to win any awards but he does have the tools to eventually become serviceable. Whether he sticks at the hot corner or not doesn't matter; it's all about the bat. There's a ton of pressure on it, but he has the physical skills to be one of the best hitters in the organization.

The Risks: High. Montero's limited defensively and has only one year above rookie ball under his belt. The quality approach he displayed in Peoria will have to translate against advanced pitching.

Ben Carsley's Fantasy Take: Annnnnnd we've already entered the flier portion of our program for fantasy. Montero's bat makes him interesting, and his lead time isn't too crazy for a dude few knew much about until reading the paragraphs above. That being said, Montero's upside isn't real high, and it's easy to imagine his defensive limitations pushing him to more of a bench-bat role. He might be a top-200 prospect, but just barely.

6 Malcom Nunez 3B   OFP: 55   Likely: 45   ETA: 2024
Born: 03/09/01   Age: 18   Bats: R   Throws: R   Height: 5'11"   Weight: 205
Origin: International Free Agent, 2018

The Report: While the Mesa brothers were the biggest names to sign out of Cuba in 2018, Nunez might be the best long term bet with the bat. We don't normally describe right-handed swings as "pretty" but his qualifies, with advanced feel for the barrel and some present raw pop which might turn into legit juice in the future. He's a potential plus hit/power combination, and that's not scouting the *"Road to the Show* on rookie mode" stat line in the Dominican. He is still just a complex league guy though and the risk here is extreme both with the bat and especially the glove. Nunez is already quite stocky—the listed height and weight look roughly accurate—and he is far from a lock to stick at this corner of the infield. Regardless, the upside in the bat is well worth keeping an eye on his development for the next, oh, half decade or so.

The Risks: Extreme. We hate ranking Dominican complex guys as a rule, so the risk factor here is gonna be top-of-the-scale.

Ben Carsley's Fantasy Take: Nunez is one of my favorite lottery tickets in the low minors, and I'd rather take a flier on him in new player drafts than any of the legion of mid-rotation college arms people start popping once the premier bats are gone. He's only a top-200 guy because of the lead time, but Nunez should be a fun one to watch.

7. Griffin Roberts   RHP

OFP: 55   Likely: 45
ETA: Late 2020 as a starter, 2019 as a reliever
Born: 06/13/96   Age: 23   Bats: R   Throws: R   Height: 6'3"   Weight: 205
Origin: Round 1, 2018 Draft (#43 overall)

The Report: Roberts was absolutely dominant his junior year at Wake Forest. He led the ACC in strikeouts, punching out 130 over 96 innings. A lot of those whiffs came off Roberts' slider, arguably the single best breaking ball in the draft class. Despite his low arm slot, he stays on top of the pitch well, and it is a potential wipeout, plus-plus offering with more consistency and refinement. He can dial the fastball up to 95, but usually works more in the low 90s as a starter, and there's the requisite, very occasional mid-80s change.

Roberts could move very quickly as a reliever on the strength of the slider, and the current repertoire, arm slot, and high-effort delivery point to a long term home in the bullpen. The Cardinals do like to stretch this type of arm out as a starter for a while, although Roberts' 2019 campaign will be delayed while he serves a 50-game suspension for a drug of abuse.

The Risks: Medium. Roberts has a major-league quality two-pitch mix right now, but right now is still a year or two away from pitching in the actual majors.

Ben Carsley's Fantasy Take: He's a Cardinals pitching prospect, so who knows? But as a rule, friends don't let friends draft reliever prospects. That's why we gotta pass on Roberts, even if he is among the more intriguing options among a group that shouldn't intrigue us.

8. Evan Mendoza   3B

OFP: 50   Likely: 40   ETA: 2020
Born: 06/28/96   Age: 23   Bats: R   Throws: R   Height: 6'2"   Weight: 200
Origin: Round 11, 2017 Draft (#334 overall)

The Report: Mendoza has a filled out, average build. He's 6-foot-2 with mostly good weight and average levers for his height. He's an average athlete due to quality body control, but he lacks quick twitch or explosive strength. Mendoza has quality hand-eye coordination, which shows itself both in the field and at the plate.

Mendoza has a compact swing and a good combination of hand-eye coordination and pitch recognition. The bat speed is just average, and he is aggressive on breaking stuff below the zone. Overall, he has the physical markers of an above-average hit tool if he can refine his plate discipline and cut down on the weak contact. He has good strength and average raw power, but the swing doesn't tap into it fully even when he gets out in front and pulls the ball. The lack of length in the swing, along with only fair bat speed, will likely limit his in-game power.

Mendoza has good hands in the field and plays a pretty clean third base. His range is limited by a lack of both quickness and foot speed, but his hands and plus arm still allow him to play an average 3B. He has good baseball instincts and likely won't have much trouble learning first base as well, if it comes to that.

The Risks: Medium. Mendoza has the physical abilities to win a bench role on an MLB roster come spring training 2019. Currently, his raw physical abilities aren't enough to overcome an overly aggressive approach that leads to weak contact and whiffs in bunches. Without improved discipline, MLB pitchers will be able to abuse the combo of a fringy approach and limited bat speed.

Ben Carsley's Fantasy Take: When your ceiling is Brian Anderson we don't have to care about you until you're playing every day.

9 Edmundo Sosa   IF

OFP: 50   Likely: 40   ETA: Debuted in 2018
Born: 03/06/96   Age: 23   Bats: R   Throws: R   Height: 5'11"   Weight: 170
Origin: International Free Agent, 2012

The Report: Sosa is a good athlete with a filled out middle infielder's frame. He has a high waist with strong muscle and strength on his glutes and core. Sosa has some quick twitch and good body control.

The swing has some length to it, but Sosa generates plus bat speed and has good feel for barrel, which allows him to make hard contact around the plate. The swing comes through the zone flat more often than not and he doesn't hit for power unless he gets to the pitch on his front foot. Sosa has average raw power, but the swing doesn't tap into it efficiently and he will likely not hit for much pop in the big leagues. Sosa often gives away plate appearances by swinging at bad pitches and gets more trigger happy the longer the plate appearance goes. Even when he recognizes spin, he'll often throw his hands out and connect weakly. The approach currently limits the profile despite the physical ability for an above-average hit tool.

Defensively Sosa has fringy range at SS with a below-average arm, but he gobbles up everything around him like a 15-year veteran. His motions and footwork are smooth and consistent and the end result is that he can hold his own at SS, even if you wouldn't want him there full time. He has the quickness for 3B and already is an above-average glove at 2B as well.

Overall, Sosa's potential is tied to how much he can tame his free swinging habits and how much power he'll tap into. It's hard to see an everyday player without significant improvement in both areas.

The Risks: Medium. Guys with overly aggressive approaches and good physical hit tools tend to be pretty overrated as a general rule. The tease of what they can do always conflicts with the product they leave on the field at the MLB level. He looks more like a depth guy than an impact talent.

Ben Carsley's Fantasy Take: Watch list at best, dropped off your watch list at worst.

10. Luken Baker 1B
OFP: 50   Likely: 40   ETA: 2021
Born: 03/10/97   Age: 22   Bats: R   Throws: R   Height: 6'4"   Weight: 265
Origin: Round 2C, 2018 Draft (#75 overall)

The Report: Baker has a pretty broad range of possible outcomes based on his health and his ability to adjust to improved competition. The offensive tools themselves are massive. His fully filled out 6'4" frame carries elite raw and explosive strength.

Baker has impressive bat speed, despite a long swing. He has above-average hand-eye coordination and has a good feel for getting the barrel on the ball. Baker has a strong understanding of the zone and doesn't chase when he recognizes the pitch. Pitchers can beat him high and in with velocity, especially if there's the threat of a good breaking ball or changeup low in the zone. Baker could also occasionally be enticed into chasing quality off-speed low.

The raw power is double-plus, if not elite, and Baker will regularly put up crazy-high exit velocity numbers. The swing is currently a bit flat and tailored for line drives, but when he gets out in front of a pitch he can hit majestic bombs.

Baker is a liability in the field, as he is flat-out slow. He can make the routine plays at 1B and has an above-average arm to make strong throws to 2B (a shame, as his arm was elite before he got hurt). Baker is locked at 1B. Baker has to hit to provide even average MLB production due to his lack of supporting tools. His power and bat speed provide a large offensive ceiling that will be limited by his ability to adjust against quality breaking stuff and limit his weaknesses up and in against velocity due to his swing length.

The Risks: Medium. He's a first baseman in the low minors. The bat better be great.

Ben Carsley's Fantasy Take: We made it about halfway through, but here is your C.J. Cron comparison: this is a C.J. Cron-ass prospect.

The Next Five:

11. Dylan Carlson OF
Born: 10/23/98   Age: 20   Bats: B   Throws: L   Height: 6'3"   Weight: 195
Origin: Round 1, 2016 Draft (#33 overall)

Getting to the Florida State League as a 19-year-old is no mean feat, and Carlson has draft pedigree to boot as the 33rd overall pick in 2017. Rany Jazayerli found that young prep picks have a huge long-term performance advantage over their older peers, so there's plenty of reason to be patient with Carlson. For ranking purposes though, this is a cohort of one, and Carlson hasn't consistently shown

St. Louis Cardinals 2019

enough bat to carry a corner outfield profile so far in his professional career. It's possible that he could, as he is a large human who makes loud contact. He's also very patient at the plate, so perhaps all of our patience will be rewarded with an everyday player. Barring that, there's enough here to be an outfield bench bat at least.

12 Daniel Poncedeleon   RHP
Born: 01/16/92   Age: 27   Bats: R   Throws: R   Height: 6'4"   Weight: 185
Origin: Round 9, 2014 Draft (#285 overall)

The latest beneficiary of Cardinals Devil Magic, the 26-year-old Poncedeleon dominated the Pacific Coast League and didn't hit many speed bumps during his late-summer call up. The stuff isn't going to wow you here, as you'd probably guess from a 26-year-old ninth-round senior sign. He works primarily off a low-90s fastball with some armside run. He can get it up to 95 and has plus command of the pitch. His cutter has more run than tilt, but coming in around 90, it's an effective armside weapon. He has a potentially average change and curve as well. Poncedeleon can be a bit hittable—despite the plus command he likes to work up in the zone a bit too much at times—but is a ready-now backend starter with upper minors and a bit of major-league success under his belt already.

13 Genesis Cabrera   LHP
Born: 10/10/96   Age: 22   Bats: L   Throws: L   Height: 6'1"   Weight: 170
Origin: International Free Agent, 2013

Cabrera was the first of two prospects sent to the Cardinals for Tommy Pham—who already is doing a grand job ingratiating himself with Rays Twitter. It's easy to think of him as a better fit for the Rays, what with The Opener™ and their subsequent willingness to more aggressively pull pitchers before the third time through the order, but it's the rare team that can't use a lefty who bumps 95 with a plus cutter/slider in his locker as well. Given Cabrera's lack of a third pitch and less than ideal command/control, he's likely to end up a late-inning reliever in St. Louis. Ironically, his best chance of "starting" was back in Tampa.

14 Randy Arozarena   OF
Born: 02/28/95   Age: 24   Bats: R   Throws: R   Height: 5'11"   Weight: 170
Origin: International Free Agent, 2016

Arozarena follows the bench outfielder recipe to a tee. If there was a baseball version of Ruhlman's Twenty, he'd be first up in the tweener chapter. Arozarena is speedy, but not so speedy, or so instinctual, that he's a regular center field option. He makes contact, but an aggressive approach can limit the quality of it. There is distinctly not enough power for a corner. Marinating time is minimal at least, as Arozarena has 300+ Triple-A plate appearances under his belt now. He's also the kind of prospect who just ends up with a carrying hit tool in St. Louis; perhaps the Cardinals Devil Magic all along was just a good finishing salt, like Himalayan pink.

15 Justin Williams OF
Born: 08/20/95   Age: 23   Bats: L   Throws: R   Height: 6'2"   Weight: 215
Origin: Round 2, 2013 Draft (#52 overall)

It seems like a lifetime ago that Arizona drafted Williams in the second round. Now on his third organization after joining Cabrera in the Pham deal, Williams still doesn't regularly tap into his impressive raw tools. He struggles with lefty spin and almost all his power comes against righties. And despite ample raw pop, he doesn't lift the ball particularly often. Like Arozarena, he is basically major-league-ready, and likely a bench outfielder. If you prefer Williams' longside platoon pop potential to Arozarena's speed and glove, fair enough. There's not much to separate the two value-wise despite very different profiles.

Others of note:

Ivan Herrera, C, GCL Cardinals

Signed out of Panama for $200,000 in 2016. Herrera came stateside this summer and mashed. His bat is generally fringy, although his defensive skills are advanced. Herrera is close to physically maxed—oh to be built like a catcher at just 18—and profiles as more of a glove-first backup for now, but if he keeps hitting it doesn't take much to lift a projection in the catching prospect market.

Seth Elledge, RHP, Double-A Springfield

Acquired from the Mariners for sinker/slider relief arm Sam Tuivailala, Elledge is a potential… sinker/slider relief arm; Jerry is going to Jerry. Tuivailala is obviously already established in the majors and Elledge is not, but he isn't that far off. There's a little less fastball here, but Elledge touches 95 with good sink and his slider flashes above-average. So yeah, he's a 95-and-a-slider guy who could help the Cardinals pen by the end of the 2019. Or get traded to the Mariners for the next sinker/slider dude down the line.

Top Talents 25 and Under (born 4/1/93 or later):

1. Jack Flaherty
2. Alex Reyes
3. Paul DeJong
4. Nolan Gorman
5. Harrison Bader
6. Tyler O'Neill

St. Louis Cardinals 2019

7. Jordan Hicks
8. Dakota Hudson
9. Andrew Knizner
10. Elehuris Montero

The Cardinals' top young player made his first full season count, turning in the best strikeout rate of any rookie starter, the second-best WHIP, and going toe-to-toe with Walker Buehler in two showstopping late-season duels. By all rights and reason, One Year Ago You would have to assume the previous sentence was about Alex Reyes fulfilling his promise, but instead it was Jack Flaherty exceeding his. Strains and tears are piling up on Reyes' track record, and with them a greater and greater chance that he'll be limited to relief or some lesser impact role.

Flaherty, meanwhile, provides something far more tangible at this point: Results. With a 94 mph fastball and a gliding slider that perfectly suits his arm angle, he was one of baseball's 25 best pitchers in 2018—all the while notching an elite zone-contact rate that indicates surprising bat-missing ability and the potential for even more down the line. For so long, Reyes was the ace of the future; that belt now belongs to Flaherty.

Paul DeJong will never be a defensive asset or on-base machine, but Air-Ball Revolution Jhonny Peralta will hit 25 dingers as sure as the sun will rise. The question, then, is whether emerging talents like Harrison Bader can surpass that contribution. Some numbers would tell you Bader already did, but defense is nearly as hard to trust as it is to measure. Not even remotely a contact hitter, Bader's baserunning and center-field prowess won't feel nearly as exciting if a sky-high .358 BABIP and 11 plunkings vanish and turn his average-ish bat into a liability.

Comparing the disparate skills and flaws of corner outfield slugger Tyler O'Neill and potential impact relievers Jordan Hicks and Dakota Hudson feels like a fool's errand, but this fool is here to try. O'Neill, by virtue of not being a relief pitcher, has the highest ceiling. In fact, his minor-league numbers and Bowflex-commercial physique suggest a chance at stardom. The issue is an out-front swing that leads to pretty significant chase issues. At various levels of the minors, he adjusted and exhibited the power that makes him interesting without striking out too often. That process is going to be more difficult in the majors, but it's certainly possible.

Already famous for his triple-digit fastballs, Hicks went through this cycle in 2018: Wildness, followed by obsessive strike-throwing, followed by more walks when hitters just started swinging. As part of that retrenchment, he used his sharp slider more, to good effect. But as the Cardinals' offseason indicates, there is work to do before we can talk about him as a relief ace.

Far less tested at the highest level, Hudson's 27 big-league innings nonetheless look a lot like his time in the minors: Extreme, nearly inexplicable overachievement featuring bushels of walks, few strikeouts, and a sparkling ERA. We know he has a dynamite slider; the rest of the arsenal will likely confine him to the bullpen. Trusting him to beat his peripherals by several runs is not something we're ready to do yet, so the potential setup man falls to the bottom of this very volatile totem pole. For now.

Part 3: Featured Articles

The Hole in The Shift is Fixing Itself

Russell Carleton

I've been on a bit of a mission against The Shift of late. I'm not out to get The Shift for the usual reasons that people oppose it. The words "the right way to play the game" won't be found on my lips. If a team wants to pursue a strategy that is within the rules and it works, then by all means, they have my blessing (not that they need it). Instead, my concern with The Shift is a worry that it doesn't work, or at least that it has a flaw that needs fixing.

The data show that while The Shift does a decent job of preventing singles on balls in play (what it's supposed to do), it also increases the number of walks that happen in front of it, and the number of additional walks outweighs the number of singles saved. It's a problem because you can't throw a guy out if he gets to walk to first base.

But the "why" was important. It seemed that The Shift was changing the way in which pitchers pitched. We saw that there were fewer fastballs thrown in front of The Shift than we might otherwise expect, and that pitchers tended to stay out of the strike zone a little more. Not by a lot. In fact, it might not even be visible to the naked eye. The percentage of pitches that are out of the zone goes from 51.0 to 53.3 from a standard defense (two right/two left) to a full shift (three on one side). That difference stands up even after we control for the types of hitters that get shifted against. And it's enough to drive up the walk rate to where it cancels out the benefits that teams thought they were getting with The Shift… and then some.

But there was some hope. I found that when individual pitchers stayed closer to the in-zone/out-of-zone mix that they used without The Shift on, they could still get the benefits of The Shift without the walk problems. So, in theory, a team could simply figure out a way to convince its pitchers to not fall prey to the walk trap and The Shift would once again be their friend.

It's reasonable to think that some teams might be more hip to this idea than others. Maybe some figured it out a year before the others. Maybe they were better at getting the message across to their pitchers. Or, maybe no one has figured it out yet.

Warning! Gory Mathematical Details Ahead!

St. Louis Cardinals 2019

I used data from 2015-2017, made available through MLB's data portal, Baseball Savant. They are kind enough to note when teams are using an infield shift (three fielders on one side of second base), as opposed to a "strategic shift" (someone's playing a bit out of position, but it's not quite that drastic) or a "standard" alignment.

Since we're doing this by team, I can't just look at raw walk rates, because we know that some teams have good pitchers and others have not-so-good pitchers. Some have a mix of both. I used the log-odds ratio method to take into account a batter's general walking proclivities, and a pitcher's as well, and then shoving them into a binary logistic regression. Then, I asked the computer to generate a specific coefficient for each team's pitchers, for when they went into The Shift and how that affected their walk rate.

Using those coefficients, I was able to project what would happen if a league-average pitcher faced a league-average hitter (which we expect would product a league-average walk rate; from 2015-2017, 7.7 percent of plate appearances ended in a walk) and then just switched his hat. Here's the top five and the bottom five:

Top 5 Teams	Projected Shift Walk Rate	Bottom 5 Teams	Projected Shift Walk Rate
Rockies	6.2%	Rangers	11.2%
Pirates	6.7%	Mets	10.4%
Indians	7.2%	Dodgers	10.2%
Astros	7.3%	Cardinals	9.9%
Braves	7.7%	Tigers	9.7%

There are probably people out there right now trying to figure out what the common thread is among the top and bottom teams. I'm sure, because this is Baseball Prospectus, people are already trying to make the case that sabermetric "early adopters" have some sort of edge here. I think that the more interesting piece is that by the time you get to fifth place in The Shift, we're at league average.

As a sanity check, I examined the issue on a pitch-by-pitch level, looking at how often pitchers threw their pitches in the GameDay strike zone, and again using the same basic methodology and getting team-specific coefficients. The names on the list re-arranged themselves, but the idea was the same, and the two lists correlated with an R of .593.

There's a reason that I don't usually do this type of leaderboard post. I don't really know what the Rockies, Pirates, Indians, Astros, and Braves have in common, or what they have that the bottom five don't. I can put a shrug emoji here and say, "Well, it must be something!" but that seems like a cop-out. Instead, I'd like to present another table and suggest that the table above doesn't even really matter anymore.

Year	League Percent Outside K Zone (Full Shift)	League Percent in K Zone (No Shift)	Difference
2015	54.1%	51.1%	3.0%
2016	53.3%	50.9%	2.4%
2017	52.6%	50.9%	1.7%
2018	52.0%	50.7%	1.3%

The hole in The Shift is fixing itself, and it's coming down really fast league wide. In my earlier work on The Shift, I suggested that until teams stopped having such a huge difference between their out-of-zone rate with and without The Shift on, there would just be too many walks for The Shift to make sense. It seems that all 30 of them have been working toward just that. I once estimated that it takes about 10 years for an idea to filter its way through baseball. At this rate, it looks like teams are going to catch up a lot faster than that. And yeah, they're all saber-smart now.

It's likely that whatever magic it was that the Rockies and Pirates had has made its way to Texas and Queens. Or is at least on its way. And if teams are committing to fixing the walk problem, then it's likely that they will continue shifting and shifting a lot.

And eventually it's going to actually make sense for them to do it.

—*Russell Carleton is a former author of Baseball Prospectus and now an analyst for the New York Mets.*

The State of the Quality Start

Rob Mains

One of the seven things you (probably) didn't know about the 2018 season is that quality starts—defined as a start lasting six or more innings with three or fewer earned runs allowed—as a percentage of total starts cratered to an all-time low of 41 percent. I want to look a little more deeply into this, since it's been a while (May of 2016, to be exact) since I've examined quality starts.

The term *quality start* is credited to *Philadelphia Inquirer* sportswriter John Lowe. It's been derided ever since he coined it in December of 1985. Three runs in six innings? That's a 4.50 ERA! In what world is that a measure of quality?

Let's start with that criticism. It's true that 3 x 9 / 6 = 4.5. (You came here for this sort of high-level math, right?) But it's also true that type of start, meeting the bare minimum for earning a quality start, is unusual. Here's the proportion of quality starts in which the pitcher lasted exactly six innings and yielded exactly three earned runs. (I'm going to confine this analysis to the 30-team era, 1998-present. Almost all data retrieved in this article is via the Baseball-Reference Play Index.)

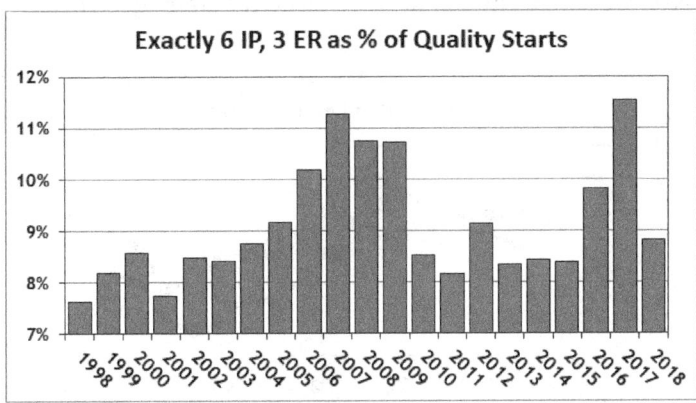

There were 1,997 quality starts in 2018. Only 176, or fewer than one in 11, featured a pitcher going six innings and allowing three earned runs. Put another way, the percentage of quality starts that resulted in a 4.50 ERA (8.8 percent) is less than half the percentage of games in which a batter hit two home runs and his team lost (22.5 percent; 237-69 won-lost). That doesn't impugn hitting two homers.

So if a 4.50 ERA isn't the norm, what is? How good are quality starts?

Pretty good, it turns out. First, on a team level:

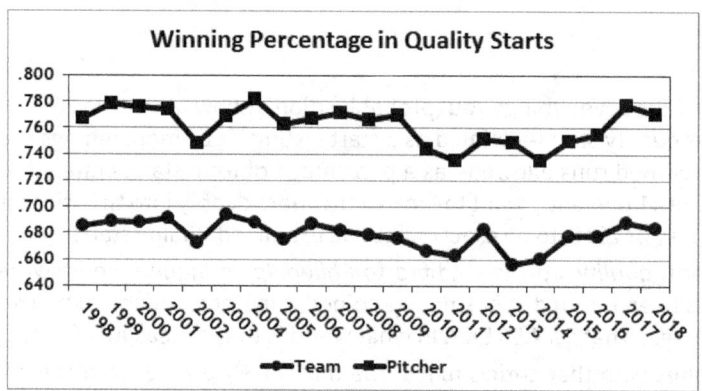

Teams receiving a quality start from their pitcher won 68.4 percent of their games in 2018, in line with the 30-team era average of 67.9 percent. A team with a .684 winning percentage wins 111 games. Getting a quality start is definitely a good thing. Individual pitchers throwing quality starts have a higher winning percentage because a big slice of team losses is assigned to a reliever.

If teams do well in quality starts, how well do the starting pitchers do? Again, very well.

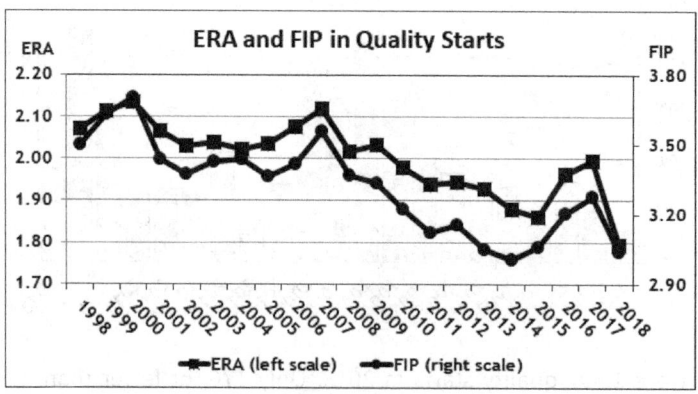

Pitchers in quality starts had a 1.79 ERA (blue line) in 2018, *the lowest in the 30-team era*. Their FIP was higher, 3.04, but still excellent. In the 30-team era, only 2014 had a lower FIP for quality starts, 3.01.

But, of course, the run environment in 2014 was different. Teams in 2014 scored 4.07 runs per game, the fewest in a non-strike year since 1976. They scored 4.45 runs per game in 2018. So surrendering a 3.04 FIP in 2018 is more impressive than 3.01 in 2014. Accordingly, let's look at ERA and FIP in quality starts relative to league averages.

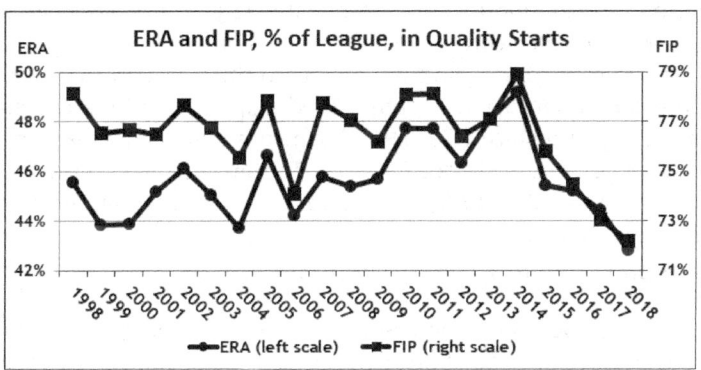

This tells a more dramatic story. Starting pitchers in 2018 gave up a 4.19 ERA and a 4.21 FIP. Starters in quality starts gave up a 1.79 ERA, 43 percent of the league average. Starters in quality starts gave up a 3.04 FIP, 72 percent of the league average. Both of these marks represent lows in the 30-team era.

The takeaway here is this: *Quality starts are better, relative to other starts, than they've ever been over the past 21 years.*

Maybe during the winter I'll look at this over a longer arc of time. For now, though, we can definitively say quality starts are the best they've ever been since the Diamondbacks and Rays joined the majors.

Yet, paradoxically, they're down.

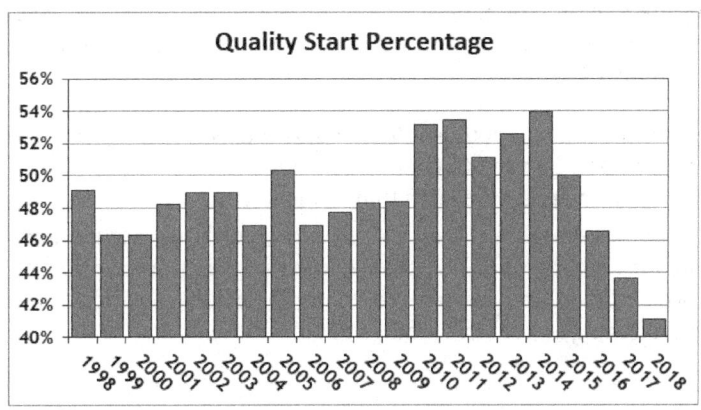

This graph covers only the 30-team era. In my article last week, though, I looked at the years 1908-2018. The result was the same. The 41 percent of starts in 2018 that were quality starts are an all-time low, well below the runners-up: 1930's 43 percent (the year teams scored an all-time record 5.55 runs per game) and last year's 44 percent.

The normal explanation for a dip in quality start percentage is an increase in scoring. When teams score a lot of runs, it's harder for starting pitchers to last six or more innings and limit opponents to three earned runs. From 1998 to 2014, the correlation between runs scored per game and the percentage of starts that were quality starts was -0.94. That means there was an extremely close relationship: More runs, fewer quality starts. Too small a sample? Go back to the start of the Expansion Era, 1961, and the relationship is even more negative, a -0.95 correlation, though 2014.

But that's broken down over the past four years:

- 2015: Runs per game increased from 4.07 to 4.25, quality start percentage decreased from 54.0 to 50.1. Yes, that's a negative relationship, but the regression model would predict a decline of 1.5 percentage points. We got 3.9 instead.
- 2016: Runs per game increased from 4.25 to 4.48, quality start percentage decreased from 50.1 to 46.6. Past experience would suggest a decline of just 1.8 percentage points. We got 3.4.
- 2017: Runs per game increased from 4.48 to 4.65, quality start percentage decreased from 46.6 to 43.6. Again, the direction's right, but the magnitude isn't. Using the relationship from 1998 to 2014, that increase in scoring should've reduced quality starts by 1.3 percentage points, not 2.9.
- 2018: Runs per game declined from 4.65 to 4.45. That should've resulted in the quality start percentage moving in the other direction, rising 1.6 points. It didn't. It fell 2.6 points, as noted, to an all-time low.

Granted, we're talking about just four years here. Maybe they're outliers. But I don't think they are. Quality starts, as noted, are as good or better than ever. But they're rarer than ever as well. And I think I know why.

To get a quality start, you need to allow three or fewer earned and pitch at least six innings. That's 18 outs. Here's a graph showing the number of starting pitchers who limited their opponents to three or fewer earned runs but got pulled after pitching at least five innings but fewer than six:

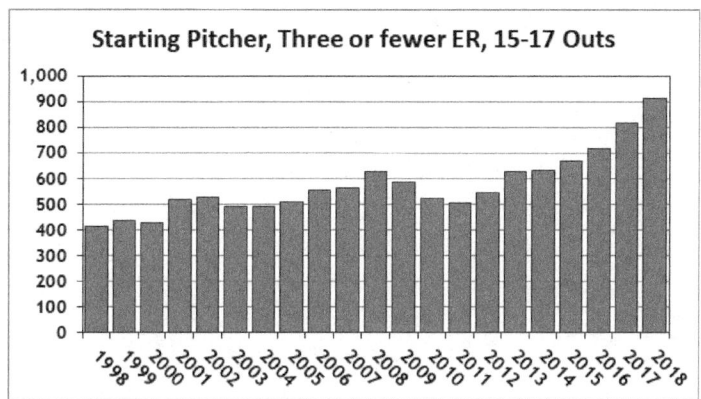

A pitcher getting 15 outs pitched five innings. A pitcher getting 16 outs pitched 5 1/3. A pitcher getting 17 outs pitched 5 2/3. More than ever before, pitchers are being removed from games in which they are within 1-3 outs of a quality start, falling just short of the six-inning finish line. Widespread acknowledgement of the times-through-the-order penalty and a flotilla of available bullpen arms is making the quality start simultaneously both more excellent and more rare.

Which is ironic, given that we saw a new post-war quality start record this season:

Rank	Pitcher	Season	Consecutive QS
1	Jacob deGrom	2018	24
2	Bob Gibson	1968	22
-	Chris Carpenter	2005	22
4	Johan Santana	2004	21
5	Luis Tiant	1968	20
-	Mike Scott	1986	20
-	Jake Arrieta	2015	20
8	Robin Roberts	1952	19
-	Tom Seaver	1973	19
-	Jack Morris	1983	19
-	Greg Maddux	1998	19
-	Josh Johnson	2010	19
-	Jon Lester	2014	19

While there have been longer streaks spread over multiple seasons, no pitcher since World War II threw more consecutive quality starts in one year than Jacob deGrom this year. The fact that he did in a year in which quality starts were the rarest they've ever been adds to the accomplishment.

—*Rob Mains is an author of Baseball Prospectus.*

Heads-Up Hacking—The First Pitch

Matthew Trueblood

Batters fell behind in a higher percentage of all plate appearances in 2018 than in any previous season for which we have pitch-by-pitch data. That kind of granular information goes back only to 1988, but we might safely assume (given all we know about baseball as it had been before that, and as it has been in the years since) that batters have *never* fallen behind at a higher rate than they did last season.

Through the 1990s, the percentage of all plate appearances that began 0-1 hovered in the high 30s and low 40s. In the 2000s, it rose steadily but slowly, through the mid-40s. In 2018, 49.8 percent of all trips to the plate began 0-1. That, as much as anything, captures in microcosm the nature of hitting in MLB today.

A countdown clock toward strike three begins ticking almost the moment a batter takes his place in the box. The league's adjusted OPS+ on the first pitch was higher in 2018 than ever before, and that has been true in most of the last 10 seasons. Batters hit .264/.289/.442 in all plate appearances in which they swung at the first pitch last season, and .241/.330/.395 in all plate appearances in which they took that first offering.

The percentage differences in batting average and isolated power there favor swinging at the first pitch by more than in any season since 1988, while the difference in on-base percentage favors taking by more than ever. If you want to get on base at a decent clip, it's a good idea to be patient, but you run the risk of missing the only chances you'll get to produce power.

St. Louis Cardinals 2019

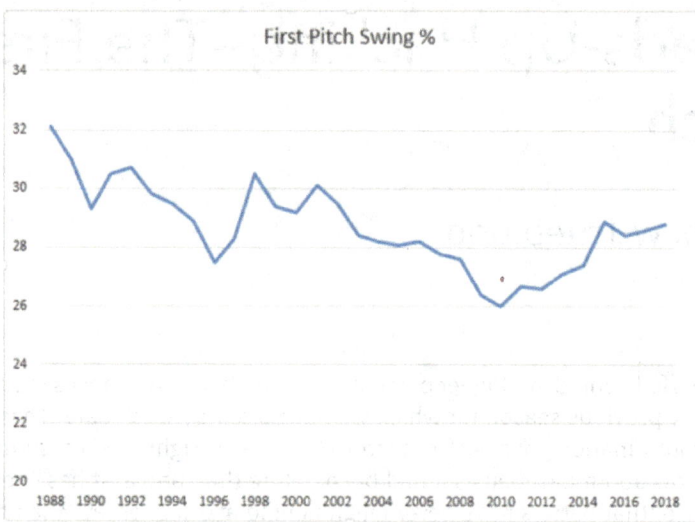

The league swung at the first pitch 28.8 percent of the time in 2018. With the isolated exception of 2015, that's the highest that number has climbed since 2002, but it might not be high enough. With the help of BP research maven Rob McQuown, I looked at the aggregate Called Strike Probability (CSProb) on the first pitch for each season since 2008, when the implementation of PITCHf/x first made measuring that possible. It's risen sharply during that period.

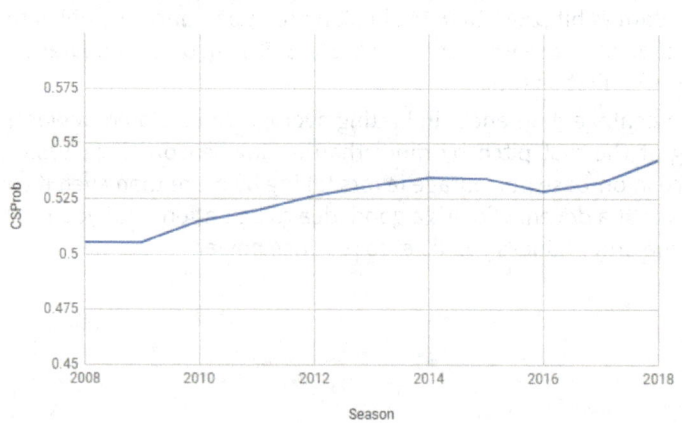

Called Strike Probability, First Pitch of PA (2008-2018)

Called Strike Probability is exactly what it sounds like: a pitch with a given CSProb has roughly that chance of being called a strike, if not swung at. In 2018, a batter who took 100 first pitches from a random sampling of the league's pitchers might expect to fall behind 54 or 55 times—up from 50 or 51 times in 2008. Almost regardless of pitch type (and, notably, especially in the case of fastballs), the first pitch tends to have more of the zone right now than ever before.

Pitchers are better at throwing strikes. They have better stuff, and believe more in their ability to miss bats within the zone. Perhaps most importantly, they know that batters are looking for one thing on the first pitch: a fastball. If they don't get it, they're likely to take the pitch. Check out how the use of sinkers and four-seamers on the first pitch has changed in a decade:

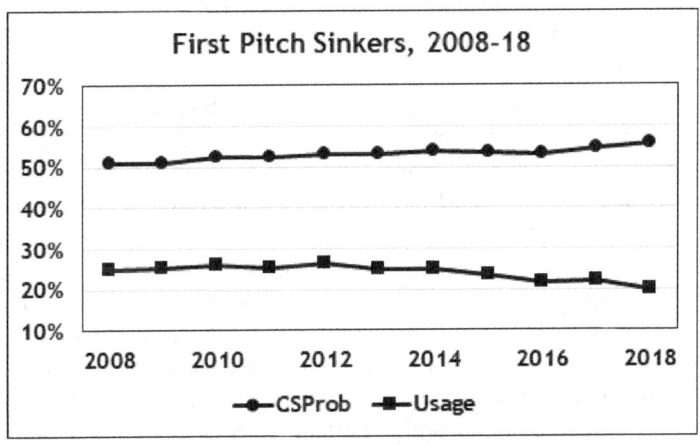

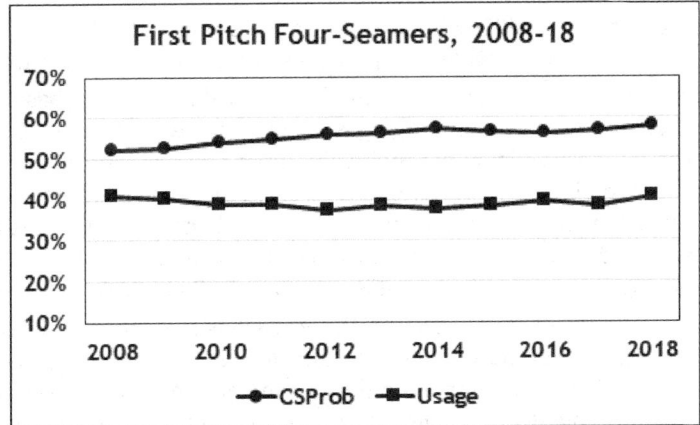

The sinker is losing its place in baseball, but the rate at which pitchers have thrown it on the first pitch hasn't dropped any faster than its usage rate in other counts. Pitchers have actually gone to their four-seamer *more* often to open counts, in the last few years, after a dip in the 2012-2015 period. What's really changed, though, and what shows up in both charts above, is that pitchers are catching more of the zone with first-pitch fastballs than they were a decade ago, or a half-decade ago. They're attacking right away, even with the pitch they know batters are expecting. The message is pretty clear: batters are being too passive.

Sliders, curves, and changeups each have more of the zone when thrown on the first pitch than they did several years ago, too, though the effect is less pronounced. Pitchers have seen the numbers; they know batters are doing better on the first pitch itself. They still feel safe throwing more and better strikes than ever before, figuring they'll come out ahead as long as they keep getting ahead to open each battle.

The Moneyball revolution brought an increased league-wide focus on OBP, which resulted in a de facto mandate to take a more patient tack at the plate. It worked very well for a while, as batters with poor plate discipline were compelled to either adjust or be expelled from the league, and pitchers with poor control were slowly weeded out.

However, concurrent with that revolution, and spurred by it in some ways, was the evolution of the pitching paradigm that now dominates the game. As batters ratcheted up their focus on inflating pitch counts and working walks, pitchers honed theirs on throwing strikes and missing bats. The league's understanding of what makes a good pitcher improved at least as much, from the mid-1990s through the mid-2000s, as its understanding of what makes a good hitter. As amphetamines and other performance-enhancing drugs were phased mostly out of the game, and as PITCHf/x broke onto the scene, individuals and teams learned how to exploit the evolved approaches of even the smartest hitters.

The ability to avoid making outs is still the most valuable one in baseball, but the magnitude of its eclipse of slugging is smaller than ever. To a greater extent than power, on-base skills derive their value from chaining—from the on-base skill levels of the players on either side of a given individual. Eleven years ago, when the housing crisis hit, people learned the hard way that the value of their homes depended a good deal on the values of their neighbors' homes. The same wasn't true, though, of their cars. So it is now, with OBP and SLG.

The global OBP in 2018 was .318. The only seasons since the Dead Ball Era in which the league got on base at a worse clip were 2013-2015, 1988, 1971-1972, and 1963-1968. This is all happening despite the aforementioned evolution of the science of hitting. It's happening despite a shift in approach and focus, one that would steer OBP ever higher, if only it were working.

Instead, it's sitting at a low ebb, and while it does so, even guys who get on base often are a little less helpful than they were 10 years ago—or 20, or 40, or 60, or 70, or 80, or 90. They're less helpful, that is, because unless there happen to be three or four other guys in the lineup who get on just as regularly, their contribution is merely to forestall the inevitable. Runs happen, increasingly, when a sudden bang happens, and that means attacking early in the count—because pitchers are sure as hell doing that.

In a league making contact on barely 75 percent of its swings, and a league in which an increasing number of pitchers can throw multiple off-speed pitches for strikes in any count, the only way to consistently generate offense is going to be aggressive. This isn't necessarily true for individuals, like Mookie Betts and Jose Ramirez, who make a lot of contact and have excellent plate discipline, and whose power comes from such natural quickness in a short stroke. Most players have to make tradeoffs, though, whether it be lowering their contact rate or raising their chase rate, in order to consistently make the quality of contact necessary to survive in today's game.

Highest %	Lowest %
Javier Baez – 48.3	Joe Mauer – 4.6
Freddie Freeman – 47.1	Mookie Betts – 9.7
Ozzie Albies – 46.3	Brett Gardner – 10.7
Jose Altuve – 44.2	Jose Ramirez – 12.0
Nick Castellanos – 44.1	Jason Kipnis – 13.8
Joey Gallo – 42.3	Jesus Aguilar – 14.5
Corey Dickerson – 40.9	Xander Bogaerts – 15.8
Salvador Perez – 40.8	Brian Dozier – 16.3
Eddie Rosario – 40.7	Mike Trout – 17.6
Nick Ahmed – 40.4	Yasmani Grandal – 17.6

Top 10 and Bottom 10 Hitters, First-Pitch Swing Rate (2018)

The question isn't which of these lists one prefers, but what they each convey, qualitatively, about the cat-and-mouse game of early-count hitting. Those top five on the left, especially, drive home the fact that for most players, getting aggressive early in the count is now key to keeping strikeout rate down and hitting for power.

For now, the message is: pitchers are coming right after batters with the nastiest stuff they've ever had. Batters had better stop giving away strike one and force hurlers to adjust, or the global OBP crisis is only going to get worse.

—*Matthew Trueblood is an author of Baseball Prospectus.*

A Hymn for the Index Stat

Patrick Dubuque

We survived without computers. I know this, because I remember the day when my dad hooked up his brand-new Atari 400 computer to the back of our 12-inch Magnavox television, and the perfect blue of the memo pad lit up for the first time. I was born just on the edge of that transitional generation, of learning cursive and balancing checkbooks and just doing math all the time, constant manual arithmetic.

It still amazes me. We learned how to sail ships without computers. We learned how to do calculus. We built towers that didn't fall down, most of the time. We engineered catapults to knock them down anyway. We built a robust system of philosophy called "utilitarianism," founded on the principle that the good of an action is evaluated by summing the effects of that action, which is the kind of formula that would make the world's mainframes crash. The whole foundation of statistics as a field is "here's math you could easily do but would die of old age first."

The fact of the matter is that there is too much math in the world to do. There are too many things changing, and too many things too small to notice, for us to handle. At some point, they become too much for the computers to handle as well, which is why we have chaos theory and undetectable earthquakes, but it's not an even fight. At some point, we fall back on intuition, and given how under-equipped we are, we're forced to bestow that intuition with some sort of supernatural superiority, the "gut feeling," that we can't prove because we can only intuit that our intuition is better.

We're all lousy at intuition, and wonderful at lying to ourselves about it. The honest truth is that computers are far better at intuition than we are, because in order to know what feels "off" you have to know what's "on." In order to do that you have to constantly reassess the average of everything, then re-rank your own experience against it.

Test your own, by comparing these three anonymous lines:

Player	G	HR	AVG	OBP	SLG
Player A	156	38	.259	.342	.535
Player B	154	38	.280	.348	.527
Player C	158	38	.266	.343	.509

These all seem like pretty similar players, right? The second one a touch more batted-ball dependent, the third a little less strong, but all pretty good hitters. And you'd be right, about the latter. Not the former.

Here's the breakdown:

- Player A: 1991 Howard Johnson, 141 DRC+
- Player B: 1996 Dean Palmer, 121 DRC+
- Player C: 2018 Giancarlo Stanton, 114 DRC+

Baseball is fortunate to have escaped the seismic shifts of so many other sports, where the talents and performances of other eras are nearly unrecognizable. (And not just other sports: try to explain the greatness of the movie Duck Soup without adjusting for era.) But they're still there, and they're nearly impossible to account for manually, without having to resort to sweeping generalizations like "steroid era" or juiced-ball era" to throw out entire swathes of production.

This is all to say that we should celebrate the index stat, that simple 100-based scale with such a humble aim: just to give context. It's hard to imagine how we lived without them for so long. Sabermetricians have always tried to make their stats look like other stats: True Average mapped to batting average, FIP molded to look like and compare to ERA. It's easy to understand the motivation—these statistics carry an emotional value in them that is hard to resist, as with the .300 hitter and the 2.00 ERA—but even they fall prey to the same loss of scale as their unadjusted counterparts. If a .300 average means different things in different years, does that hold true for a .300 True Average?

Instead, 100 doesn't say anything, except above average or below. And it does it instantly, for every season in every run environment for any statistic we want it to. We should have more index stats: K%+, so we can stop comparing Mike Clevinger's career 9.46 K/9 to Nolan Ryan's 9.55. HBP%+, so we can note that Ron Hunt was getting plunked when nobody else was getting plunked, as opposed to that imitator Brandon Guyer. Some might note how stale these references are and accuse league-adjustment as a backward-looking drive, and this is true. But we're always looking backward, always comparing the new with the expectations already set. The index stat just forces us to be honest.

There's always resistance to a new statistic, especially one so outwardly simple and so internally complex. We tend to stick with what we know, even in the case of formulas that are supposed to tell us what we know. But if your resistance is that it seems too complicated, too counterintuitive, too "black boxy," I encourage you to consider why you feel that way. Because the real world is infinitely more complicated than baseball, where all the pitches go in one basic direction and the baserunners are only allowed to travel in four directions. Baseball statistics based on mixed methodology are almost impossibly intricate. So are skyscrapers and automobiles. That's why we have computers—to take the guesswork out of them.

—*Patrick Dubuque is an author of Baseball Prospectus.*

Index of Names

Arozarena, Randy 78, 104
Bader, Harrison 20
Baker, Luken 93, 103
Brebbia, John 48
Cabrera, Genesis 88, 104
Capel, Conner 93
Carlson, Dylan 79, 103
Carpenter, Matt 22
Cecil, Brett 94
DeJong, Paul 24
Elledge, Seth 89, 105
Fernandez, Junior 94
Flaherty, Jack 50
Fowler, Dexter 26
Gallegos, Giovanny 94
Gant, John 52
Garcia, Adolis 80
Goldschmidt, Paul 28
Gomber, Austin 54
Gonzalez, Derian 94
Gorman, Nolan 81, 97
Gregerson, Luke 56
Gyorko, Jedd 30
Helsley, Ryan 90
Herrera, Ivan 93, 105
Hicks, Jordan 58
Hudson, Dakota 60, 98
Hudson, Joe 93
Knizner, Andrew 82, 99
Leone, Dominic 62
Machado, Jonatan 93
Martinez, Carlos 64
Martinez, Jose 32
Mayers, Mike 94
Meisinger, Ryan 94
Mendoza, Evan 101
Mikolas, Miles 66
Miller, Andrew 68
Molina, Yadier 34
Montero, Elehuris 83, 99
Munoz, Yairo 36
Nunez, Malcom 84, 100
O'Neill, Tyler 38
Oviedo, Johan 94
Ozuna, Marcell 40
Pena, Francisco 93
Perez, Delvin 85
Poncedeleon, Daniel 70, 104
Reyes, Alex 91, 97
Roberts, Griffin 92, 101
Robinson, Drew 42
Schrock, Max 93
Shreve, Chasen 72
Sosa, Edmundo 93, 102
Urias, Ramon 86
Wacha, Michael 74
Wainwright, Adam 76
Webb, Tyler 94
Wieters, Matt 44
Williams, Justin 87, 105
Wong, Kolten 46
Woodford, Jake 94

St. Louis Cardinals 2019

Ynfante, Wadye 93

Ballpark diagrams for Baseball Prospectus are created by THIRTY81Project, a design concept offering original ballpark artwork, including the new 'Ballparks of 2019' 11 x 17 color print.

Visit **www.thirty81project.com** for full details.

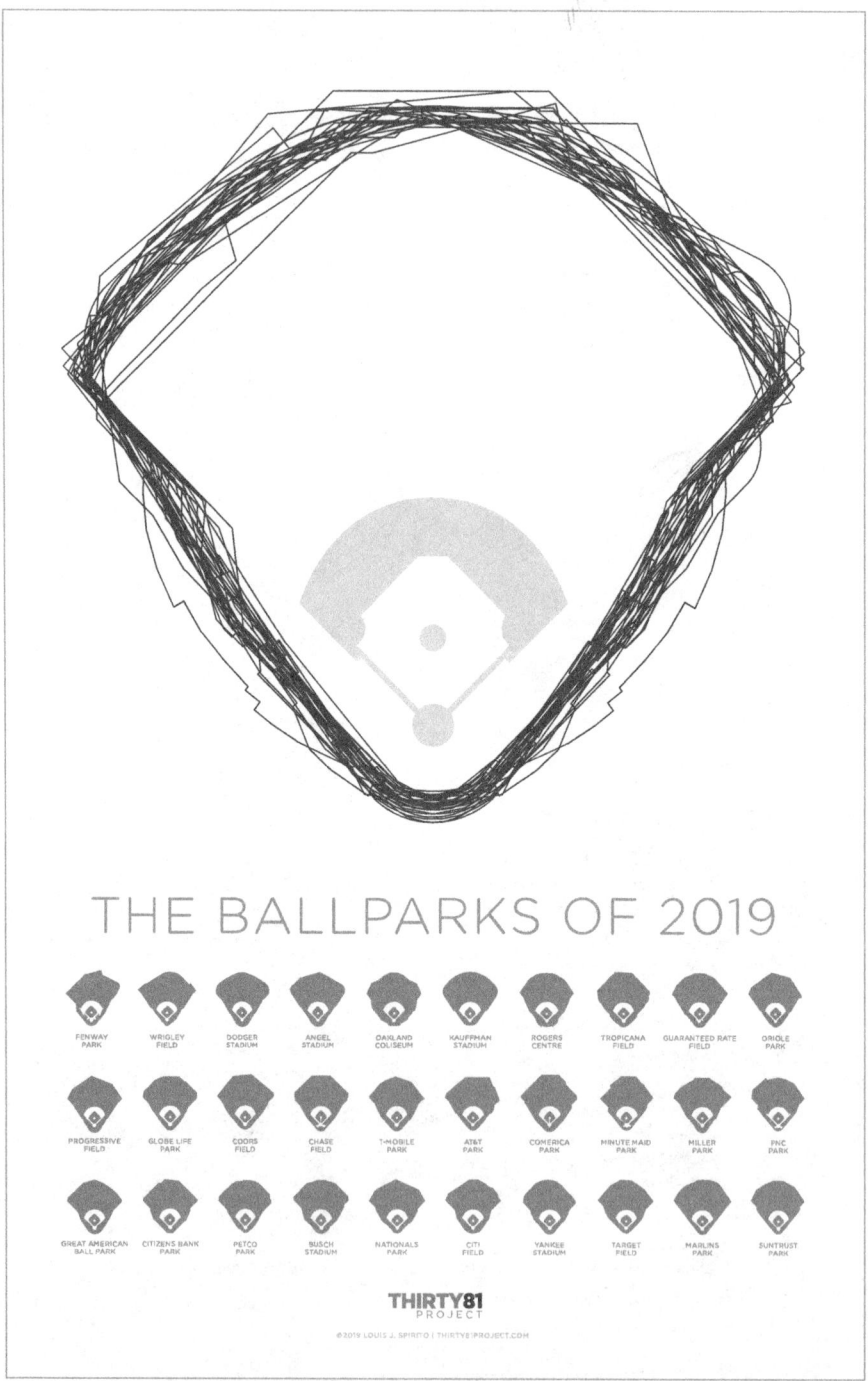